Prophecy in a Secular Age

Prophecy in a Secular Age

AN INTRODUCTION

Edited by
DAVID TRUE

PICKWICK *Publications* • Eugene, Oregon

PROPHECY IN A SECULAR AGE
An Introduction

Copyright © 2021 Wipf and Stock Publishers. All rights reserved. Except for brief quotations in critical publications or reviews, no part of this book may be reproduced in any manner without prior written permission from the publisher. Write: Permissions, Wipf and Stock Publishers, 199 W. 8th Ave., Suite 3, Eugene, OR 97401.

Pickwick Publications
An Imprint of Wipf and Stock Publishers
199 W. 8th Ave., Suite 3
Eugene, OR 97401

www.wipfandstock.com

PAPERBACK ISBN: 978-1-5326-6925-5
HARDCOVER ISBN: 978-1-5326-6937-8
EBOOK ISBN: 978-1-5326-6939-2

Cataloguing-in-Publication data:

Names: True, David, editor.

Title: Prophecy in a secular age : an introduction / edited by David True.

Description: Eugene, OR : Pickwick Publications, 2021 | Includes bibliographical references.

Identifiers: ISBN 978-1-5326-6925-5 (paperback) | ISBN 978-1-5326-6937-8 (hardcover) | ISBN 978-1-5326-6939-2 (ebook)

Subjects: LCSH: Secularization (Theology). | Eschatology. | Prophecies. | Prophecy. | Religions.

Classification: BL500 .P76 2021 (print) | BL500 .P76 (ebook)

FEBRUARY 2, 2021

Scripture quotations are from Revised Standard Version of the Bible, copyright © 1946, 1952, and 1971 National Council of the Churches of Christ in the United States of America. Used by permission. All rights reserved worldwide.

Dedicated to

Ellen and Abby

I will pour My spirit upon all flesh,
and your sons and your daughters shall prophesy.
 —JOEL 3:1, ROBERT ALTER'S INTERPRETATION

Contents

Acknowledgments | ix

Introduction —*David True* | xi

1. Reframing the Prophetic Imagination: The Hebrew Bible and American Prophecy in a Secular Age —*Amy Merrill Willis* | 1

2. Civil Religion and Prophecy Revisited —*George Shulman* | 25

3. The Revolutionary as Prophet: Imagining New Futures, Theorizing "What Could Have Been," and Rejecting the Ways of the World —*Roberto Sirvent and Andrea Smith* | 46

4. Wanting Prophecy: Prophetic Storytelling at the End of a Way of Life —*John Elia* | 59

5. Post-Katrina Prophecies —*Lisa Woolley* | 73

6. The Prophet Samuel R. Delany —*Vincent W. Lloyd* | 90

7. Secular Prophecy and the Name of God —*Tom James* | 109

Bibliography | 129

List of Contributors | 137

Acknowledgments

THIS COLLECTION IS THE work of many hands or voices, all of whom have taught me so much and done so with a grace that I aspire to emulate. Ted Smith and Amy Merrill Willis were the ones who first got me thinking that what started as a lecture series could be transformed into a manuscript. Great thanks to Wilson College for hosting the Orr Forum and the Common Hour that made for a campus-wide lecture series on prophecy as well as for granting me a semester to study with the aid of the Drusilla Stevens Mazur Research Award. Along with Amy Merrill Willis, George Shulman gave me a sense that the book could serve as an introduction to prophecy but also more specifically to prophecy in a secular age. I have learned so much from both Amy and George about a subject I had imagined I knew all there was to know.

The idea for the book developed with the lectures of John Elia, Lisa Woolley, and Vincent Lloyd. Each of them focused on secular sources that taught me to look for prophecy in unexpected places. Roberto Sirvent and Andre Smith challenged my own reformist assumptions and got me thinking about the origins, sources, and the possibilities of prophecy. Finally, Tom James taught me that prophecy is so often inspired by love as desire.

All this is a long way from my adolescent self who played John the Baptizer in a youth group musical, but perhaps not so far. In any case, that's my first memory of prophetic spirit. Thank you, Connie Stinson, for awakening a bit of that fire in me. And thanks to my parents Ron and Patty for embodying that spirit and introducing me to it in the community called First Southern. I owe so much to one of my first mentors, Tilden Bridges, and my professor Linda McKinnish Bridges for nurturing in me a fascination with the biblical prophets. It was with professors Doug Ottati and

Acknowledgments

Charles Swezey that I began to study in earnest the history of prophecy and its modern exponents like Martin Luther King. I have loved continuing this study with students at Wilson College, especially veterans of the MLK Travel Seminar like Patty Hall, Stephanie Peebles, Morgan Shadle, and Rachel Stoner. Working with so many great students and my colleagues in Philosophy and Religion, John Elia and Diane Morgan, has been an absolute joy. Diane is an extraordinary copy editor and even better friend. The third floor of Warfield hasn't been the same since Diane left.

None of this would have been accomplished were it not for my partner Ellen and our daughter Abby. In sermons and in conversations, they have taught me that prophecy can be both wise and inspired by a love stronger than death.

Introduction

Prophecy in a secular age may appear, on the surface at least, to be a logical contradiction. Prophecy is a religious phenomenon—isn't it? And isn't a secular age by definition a non-religious age? If this is a secular age, then surely prophecy belongs to a bygone era. Or if prophecy's not entirely a thing of the past, it has been argued, it remains as mere fragments.[1] We are only too familiar with angry televangelists and their reaction against the secular—a condemnation of our supposed godless age. There is a long history of such figures in American history; they have been a constant in the rise of the reactionary politics of the last half century.[2] Today, however, preachers like Franklin Graham seem little more than priests to the Oval Office, sacralizing the rule of Republican Presidents. The essays in this collection remind us that the practice of prophecy encompasses more than predicting the future or commenting on society. Indeed, they suggest that prophecy is alive and well in our secular age—and that it is poignant, powerful, and plural.

There are, of course, many introductions to the topic of prophecy. Most of them are written for fellow humanists or co-religionists.[3] This book, on the other hand, is intended for a broader audience: people working in the humanities, students and scholars, and those in ministry or preparing for it. The contributors to this collection suggest that prophecy is capable of transgressing conventional boundaries such as religious/political, believer/nonbeliever, Christian/Jew, and church/academy. Before saying more about the power of prophecy, however, I need to say a few words about what I mean by "secular."

1. West, *Prophetic Fragments*.
2. Mathewes and Nichols, *Prophecies of Godlessness*; Murphy, *Prodigal Nation*.
3. For further discussion of the expansive literature, see the first two essays in this volume.

Introduction

By "secular" I have in mind something akin to Charles Taylor's usage in his *Secular Age*. Taylor claims that modern culture is secular not in the sense that it is devoid of religion or even that religion is marginalized. He argues that modern persons find their identities contested or challenged by the existence of other, competing identities. The experience of being challenged can be variously interpreted as enriching and complementing or relativizing and threatening. Taylor concludes that modern "selves" attempt to insulate or "buffer" themselves against interference. Our situation is marked by the reality that no cultural identity holds a secure and unchallenged position, either religious or secular. Gone are the days of an assumed or secure Protestant or even Christian cultural identity.

This is not to suggest that Protestantism or Christianity more broadly does not continue to inform or haunt American culture, simply that many other identities now sit alongside it. There are parts of America that feel anything but secular—in the sense being described. I recall places I have lived in which evangelical Protestantism was still culturally prominent, with many Protestant churches dotting the landscape and gigantic crosses and American flags planted along the interstate. These places can give the impression that a single way of life still prevails. The reality is more complicated. In one such place, there was a large university and medical school that added a small but significant amount of diversity to the community. I suspect that the large crosses and flags were there in part because their owners had felt threatened, even menaced, by the very diversity that others found liberating and alive with possibility.

A growing body of evidence attests that the plurality of identities and the attendant sense of "having options" runs deep.[4] Perhaps though, the strongest testimony is our personal experience of plurality. Social media and other modern means of communication are obvious sources of our awareness of the proliferation of plural identities. Such media (along with older forms of entertainment and art) help explain the penetration of plurality into even the most remote corners of America. Americans, especially millennials and Generation Zers, are increasingly aware of multiple ways of life not simply because of their phones but because of their experience within their families and peer relationships.

If traditional religion is decentered and identities are contested, what form does prophecy take? The answer may surprise us. Rather than our secular age spelling the demise or reduction of prophecy, the works in this

---

4. Putnam and Campbell, *American Grace*, 260–320.

Introduction

collection suggest prophecy itself has pluralized, and pluralization may in turn serve to amplify prophecy to the extent that our secular age is ironically a prophetic one. If one is listening, there does seem to be something of a cacophony of prophetic voices, which raises the question of what counts as prophecy? How are we to distinguish prophecy from other forms of communication?

No one collection can hope to definitively answer that question. Prophecy extends beyond any single tradition and is much too expansive to be wrapped up for all times and places. Instead of delivering a definitive theory of prophecy, the first three essays in this volume serve as an opening conversation about prophetic traditions and sources, biblical, American, and indigenous. Biblical scholar Amy Merrill Willis initiates the conversation by breaking open and unpacking the biblical tradition. Starting with Moses and his sister Miriam, Merrill Willis uncovers multiple ways of being prophetic biblically. Her essay challenges the assumption that to be prophetic is primarily to be confrontational. Merrill Willis focuses on prophetic vision as the underlying catalyst for interpreting, engaging, and sometimes confronting the present.

Political theorist George Shulman returns to the jeremiad tradition and traces its continuing power to challenge cultural self-denial and speak truth to who we are as a people. Shulman asks what we should make of Barack Obama, who invokes the progressive nationalism of civil religion but avoids the scorching irony and critical judgements that characterize American prophecy at its best.

Religious studies scholar Roberto Sirvent and Ethnic Studies scholar Andrea Smith argue that the possibilities of the past, so often associated with nostalgia, can serve as a prophetic source of insight. Drawing on recent work in American Studies, Sirvent and Smith argue that the seemingly simple phrase, "what could have been," has the power to disrupt the sense of inevitability that the present so often holds. In freeing us from a naturalized present, the possibilities of the past open us to the possibilities of the future, possibilities that others may deem impossible.

These opening essays remind us that prophecy is a way of seeing, a perspective, an interpretative vision. A prophetic vision emerges in response to a crisis that threatens the community. In this sense, prophecy is a form of protest against the propagators of crisis who attempt to deny responsibility by dismissing the crisis, its cause(s), and their role in causing it. Where the powerful seek to maintain the status quo, prophecy sees the normal as a

Introduction

dead end. Prophecy challenges our assumptions about how things work, puncturing our confidence in our projections of progress. It sees the danger of the community's present path and calls on the community or a subset of the community to make profound change, to adopt a new course, and in so doing to create an alternative and promising future.

Prophecy is often troubling, disturbing, and even dangerous. Those in power owe their position to the current system, and thus they often see prophecy as a threat to their power, their political, cultural, and economic hegemony, or their profits. In our modern secular age, the powerful are variously conceived as "the 1%," the wealth of the top 10 percent, or as a significant political constituency. However, we conceive of the powerful, the point is that powerful people are interested or invested in the present order, be it for material or ideological reasons.

This raises a profound problem. How can prophecy gain a hearing from the powerful rather than simply being dismissed as illegitimate or demonized as "other"? The problem is further complicated by a host of challenges that include such things as partisanship, confirmation bias, information silos, etc. The problem is an old one, of course, and calls to mind other times of great social conflict, in which prophecy occurs. Prophecy is often said to overcome opposition and gain a hearing by turning to a higher authority. This, we are told, is what makes prophecy prophecy—speaking in the name of God. But what can this mean or deliver in a secular age?

The claim of this collection is that the persuasive power of prophecy is in the prophet's creative reworking of a common or shared authority—though not necessarily a canonical or traditional authority. In a traditional religious culture, a prophet might appeal to a religious narrative and accompanying beliefs. Frederick Douglass, for instance, appealed to the prophetic traditions of Isaiah and Jeremiah, the Exodus story, and Jesus to condemn the slave system of the United States.[5] His employment of a sacred history, however, went far beyond simply reciting divine commands. He connected the sacred history with his own history as a former runaway slave to offer a personal testimony that included intimate details and a cosmic sweep in which Douglass interpreted the American story anew. That is, Douglass drew on Scripture and his own experience to reinterpret our history and charge it with meaning. For Douglass this entailed a divine purpose for the nation. With the revivals of the Second Great Awakening in mind, one can hear an altar call in Douglass's appeal to his fellow citizens and the nation

---

5. Blight, *Frederick Douglass*, 228–38.

Introduction

more broadly. Douglass's rhetorical engagement with the biblical tradition served to legitimize and sacralize his call to abolish slavery. Yet, religion failed to unite the country in abandoning the slave economy. The slave power in the country refused to heed the prophet's call.

Perhaps because of this, prophets in a democratic context often turn to the nation's founding documents, especially the Declaration of Independence, with its mention of God and high ideals such as natural rights and equality. Might these words provide a shared authority? Douglass argued that the spirit animating these documents, like the biblical witness, was the equal dignity of all people. A century later, we find Martin Luther King making a similar move--appealing to Christianity and "the deep wells of democracy" in support of equal dignity.

Today such a strategy seems almost naive. The documents are as likely to divide us as they unite us. The reality is that competing "collective memories" of these documents and their attendant histories diverge dramatically from one another. For some, these documents speak of exceptional men who by their genius created an exceptional nation. Others remember the writers and signers as slave owners who were intent on preserving their power. My interest here is not in parsing these documents or their interpretative communities but in being realistic about the challenges confronting prophetic appeals to them.

If a secular age is characterized by plural and contested identities, the *American* secular age is one of agonistic struggle. A powerful constituency alarmed at social change, including pluralization, has embraced white nationalism. Gone is any sense of a shared sacred covenant or the related notion of a shared ideology or civil religion. While some may mourn and others rejoice such a development, the prospects for a national prophetic witness appear to be minimal. There are simply too many identities for any single prophet to speak to them all. If prophecy is to flourish, it must do so absent a national covenant.

Perhaps the larger Civil Rights struggle provides us with a clue. If we recall Malcolm X with Martin Luther King, we may remember that it was never one prophetic voice speaking to a united movement. Long before the Black Panther Party emerged there were tensions between ostensibly allied organizations such as the NAACP, the Southern Christian Leadership Council, and the Student Nonviolent Coordinating Committee. This history should disabuse us of fixating on Martin King as if he were the last great prophet, and now the age of prophets has closed. Prophets are, after

INTRODUCTION

all, human beings, like you and me, and yet, prophets do possess something akin to divine vision. In retelling stories, they help us see our story anew, breaking through denial with a form of truth telling that inspires us to pursue radical change.

This collection of essays traces the movement of the prophetic spirit across multiple forms and directed to diverse communities and in some cases across communities. Philosopher John Elia is interested in the possibility that prophecy might generate the social empathy needed (and missing) if we are to make the structural changes necessary to confront climate change. Elia reimages works of art as prophetic performances that might perform the affective work that politics (no longer) seems capable of doing--of opening us to the plight of others and creating possibilities of solidarity across boundaries and borders.

Literary scholar Lisa Woolley is interested in the prophetic power of secular stories, specifically the power of stories to help us improvise new ways to lament devastating loss in the wake of natural disasters. Mining the novels *Hold It 'Til It Hurts* and *Salvage the Bones*, Woolley highlights how we struggle to come to terms with the tragic, finding in social lament a neglected element of prophecy, one that ironically might help the survivors and the nation begin to heal.

Scholar of religion, Vincent Lloyd finds a critical and hopeful vision of community in reading science fiction writer Samuel Delany from the context of the Black Lives Matter movement. Focusing on Delany's three memoirs, Lloyd finds prophetic insight from what might be viewed as unlikely sources such as Delany's reflections on time spent in communal living and adult theaters.

Theologian Tom James concludes the collection by asking if there is a prophetic role for theology in a secular age. He identifies three types of prophecy in relation to the secular: theological anti-secularism, secular prophecy, and prophetic theology. The typology itself is sure to enlighten and provoke, but it is the third form with its sightings of traces of the divine in politics that raises the greatest prophetic possibilities and questions. Might it be that prophetic theology discerns the spirit of God, as it were, moving in our midst to destroy and create?

While the essays feature different prophets and approach prophecy from different perspectives, they share an agenda or vision that might be described broadly as left-of-center. What should we make of this? In part, no doubt, this shared perspective is owing to my editorial bias. Certainly, a

Introduction

different editor would have produced a different collection. I suspect, however, that something deeper is at work, something owing to the nature of prophecy itself. Since prophets protest a crisis precipitated by the powerful, prophecy tends to be seen as marginal. This is true even of those "conservative" prophecies that draw on traditional authorities like Jeremiah, Jesus, or the U.S. Constitution. In contrast, the powerful tend to operate without the aid of prophets, preferring propagandists and priests who cloak the powerful in the symbols of the sacred, thus contributing to the delegitimization of traditional religious authorities. Ironically, in using religion in this way, they appear to be further undermining the legitimacy of traditional religion and thus contributing to the secular character of our age, and, we might hope, turning our attention to the true prophets among us. My hope for this collection is that it might itself not only examine prophetic cultural phenomena but that it might bear something of the prophetic.

If this strikes the reader as a bold claim, my sense is that this is owing in part to how far removed we are from the prophetic traditions of the past. There is a temptation to think of prophecy as belonging to an enchanted world, but what if prophetic traditions speak to who we are as human beings? What if prophecy emerges from the human condition of longing, longing for truth-telling that helps us lament tragic loss, confront injustice, and envision a new world? Might it be that such longings and the practice of prophecy itself aren't simply ancient customs but are instead resident possibilities in many if not every culture?

As an artistic expression of human longing and vision, prophecy is a field of study in the humanities, but might it be more than this to the humanities? Instead of being marginalized by humanities scholars and disciplines, might prophecy speak to the very purpose of the humanities? The call for sharing stories from the margins has been reenergized and prophets tend, of course, to speak from the margins. This helps explain their longing and their distinctive vision. Might it be that we should come to see the humanities as a form of prophecy? The pragmatic voice inside my head sounds the warning bells of job security. "Stick to the script!" it commands. Yes, by now we have all heard the utilitarian defenses of the humanities with their mantras about building skills and landing jobs. I suppose such defenses may have their place, but alone they are unlikely to save the humanities. Indeed, they are likely to reduce the humanities to an adjunct of the curriculum, adjacent to and complementing the real action. Perhaps such a marginal fate is fitting a prophetic academic discipline. The

Introduction

humanities have always had a prophetic purpose—to challenge students to see the present as historical rather than natural or divine, to discover in narratives the truth about others and ourselves, to reason beyond conventions of denial and instead lament the oppressive and tragic, to long for and envision a new world. If this sounds like the work of faith communities, might we say then that the humanities have a kind of faith—a prophetic faith that sees from and beyond the margins?

1

Reframing the Prophetic Imagination

The Hebrew Bible and American Prophecy in a Secular Age

Amy Merrill Willis

The Problem with Prophecy

WHEN I TEACH THE prophets to undergraduates, I like to begin by asking my students what I need to do to be a prophet when I grow up. The question usually elicits a mix of soft chuckles and puzzled looks. This is because it makes assumptions with which my students, who are typically middle-class, white, and from mainline Christian backgrounds, cannot agree. Most of them do not think of "prophet" as a legitimate career option, much less one that I could prepare for through any formal means. My students might also suspect that I am ineligible because of my gender; after all, all of the major prophetic voices in the biblical text are male. Students are also stymied by the lack of a clear parallel between the office or role of the prophet in the Hebrew Bible, where prophecy appears as a distinct institution, and our own cultural context where prophecy seems to be disconnected from social institutions. Most of my students are fairly convinced that prophets are a thing of the past—a cultural and religious role that ceased with John the Baptist, or maybe Muhammad.

Even though my students are not sure that prophecy still exists, they will concede that there might be *prophetic* voices among us who are like the prophets in some undefined way. "How do you recognize them?" I ask. They offer various criteria, often determined by their religious formation. Religiously conservative students might mention the ability to predict the future and to work miracles, a reference to their experiences with faith-healing. Still others prefer the idea that prophetic voices mediate God's word, but they are not sure what that might entail. When I ask for particular examples, the responses are wildly divergent. Reverend Martin Luther King is almost always named. My students admire his civil rights activism, though they are remarkably unfamiliar with his religious motivations. But in the same conversation someone will also suggest the kind of preachers who are the exact opposite of King. Like Preacher Gary.

Preacher Gary is part of a national phenomenon dubbed "campus preachers." These are men who travel to public universities across the nation to preach to students.[1] Gary Birdsong has been a regular feature at the University of North Carolina in Chapel Hill since the 1980s. For decades, students there (including my husband, who graduated in 1990) have referred to him as "the pit preacher" because every fall he comes to a particularly busy spot on campus near the student center called "the pit." From there he holds forth on the sins of college students—especially college women. He and the other campus preachers have a reputation for being especially virulent. Preacher Gary shouts out to sorority women who are walking by and calls them whores. He condemns "cheerleaders in ungodly outfits," feminists, Muslims, Jews, Catholics, homosexuals, people who drink, and women who wear pants or work outside the home.[2] He utilizes heated debate to exhort all to repent lest they face a fiery and eternal future in hell. He has been banned from campus at least twice during the last thirty years for creating conflict. When he comes to campus, some students welcome him but most ignore or mock him.[3]

---

[1]. Carolina Alumni Review, "Pit Preacher Moves Off His Stage"; Lopez, "Campus Preachers."; Fornoff, "Gary Birdsong."

[2]. Fornoff, "Gary Birdsong," para. 17. If there are women among the ranks of the campus preachers, I am not aware of them.

[3]. Fornoff, "Gary Birdsong"; Lopez, "Campus Preachers."

Although Preacher Gary is a caricature of prophetic judgment, his effect on his hearers points to a larger reality named by biblical scholar Ellen Davis. Davis argues that while Americans will refer to culturally edgy and unconventional messages as "prophetic," we tend to view any religiously motivated public discourse as unsafe.[4] She remarks, "Anyone who uses prophetic language with avowed religious motivation . . . in ways that create direct pressure in contemporary situations—such a person is suspect to many or most, including the majority of Christians. (Although Martin Luther King might seem to be an exception now, he was not during his lifetime.)"[5] As a result of their deep suspicion of religious language, most Americans, my students included, prefer to confine religious forms of prophecy to the past.

Despite this desire, scholars of American rhetoric and politics acknowledge that prophetic activity continues to be a force in the present, though it is diminished and problematic.[6] For many of these scholars, prophecy is synonymous with a particular kind of religious rhetoric, the jeremiad. As the literary progeny of the Israelite prophet Jeremiah, the strident language of the jeremiad indicts audiences for collective wrongdoing in order to motivate reform. In this respect, the scholarly focus on the jeremiad—especially in the work of George Shulman[7] and Cathleen Kaveny[8]—is consistent with my students' intuitions. Martin Luther King is regarded as an extraordinary practitioner of the jeremiad, while Preacher Gary engages in what might be described as an abusive variation of it.[9]

Thus, in characterizing prophecy in the American experience, there seems to be a burgeoning gap not only between the past and the present, but also between the rhetorical power and moral heroism of Reverend King and the sexist, fundamentalist vitriol of Preacher Gary. That gap is not bridged by the common conception that prophecy is fundamentally about "speaking truth to power"[10]—the thin thread that connects King

---

4. Davis, *Biblical Prophecy*, xii.
5. Davis, *Biblical Prophecy*, xii.
6. I am referring here to West, *Prophetic Fragments*, ix-xi; Bercovitch, *American Jeremiad*; Shulman, *American Prophecy*; Kaveny, *Prophecy without Contempt*.
7. Shulman, *American Prophecy*.
8. Kaveny, *Prophecy without Contempt*.
9. Kaveny, *Prophecy without Contempt*, 286-307.
10. Sharp, *Old Testament Prophets*, 3n1, offers a brief history of this phrase, which was coined by the Quaker pacifist movement and adopted and popularized by minister and activist William Sloane Coffin.

and Preacher Gary. Undoubtedly, confrontational truth-telling in the form of social critique is a fundamental task of prophets past and present, one which Michael Walzer describes as a public act of a lone voice dressing down the powerful in the presence of the disadvantaged and the powerless.[11] However, this particular conception of prophecy has become problematic in contemporary American life. On the one hand, this confrontation is often little more than ineffective posturing or "nagging people about social justice."[12] But strident indictments under the guise of truth-telling have also become an excuse for abusive and sexist rhetoric from fundamentalist Christian speakers. In short, prophecy is not the same thing as social critique.[13] Scholars who use the Bible for political and cultural theorizing tend to privilege confrontational speech as the quintessential prophetic act, and this has been the primary way in which prophecy has been enacted and perceived in American culture. But the limitations of this conception of prophecy can be critiqued on the basis of both the biblical tradition and the challenges posed by the current context.

The Prophetic Imagination in the Immanent Frame

In his pioneering book *The Prophetic Imagination*, Walter Brueggemann, drawing on the work of rabbi-scholar-activist Abraham Joshua Heschel, argued that prophecy should be identified first and foremost with a certain kind of consciousness rather than a particular activity.[14] This consciousness is most clearly evident in the Mosaic traditions, which Brueggemann contrasted with Israel's dominant culture. According to Brueggemann, prophetic consciousness was, and is, characterized by a certain kind of imagination enabling one to see beyond current social realities and envision what could be.[15] Prophetic imagination constitutes an alternative way of knowing and compels an alternative way of living in the world. Although the surrounding culture frequently resists the prophetic vision and finds it

---

11. Walzer, *In God's Shadow*, 78.

12. Gilbert, "What Does It Mean to Be Prophetic Today?" 12:08–10. Brueggemann also asserted the distinction between social critique and prophetic activity in his groundbreaking work, *Prophetic Imagination*, 2–3.

13. Brueggemann, *Prophetic Imagination*, 3.

14. Brueggemann, *Prophetic Imagination*, 3. Brueggemann's discussion of prophetic consciousness is indebted to Heschel, *Prophets*, ix–xv.

15. Brueggemann, *Prophetic Imagination*, xiv–xv.

shocking, it does not necessarily require direct confrontation with dominant culture.[16]

The prophetic imagination takes on further significance in the context of our secular age. Charles Taylor contends that our experience of secularism should not be defined as the absence of religion, but as the circumstance of being able to choose belief. In our secular age, belief is contested, but not gone.[17] This co-existence of belief and unbelief can manifest itself in quite robust ways; so it is not really the case that the secular age is one in which belief has simply been corroded by skepticism, materialism, and selfishness.[18] Instead, Taylor invites us to consider how our contemporary worldview, which he dubs the immanent frame, undergirds the dynamic interplay between belief and unbelief. The immanent frame complicates our apprehension of prophecy because it convinces us that the cosmos is rational and non-mysterious. The Israelite prophets lived within a world that was thought to be embedded within a larger cosmos and shaped by bigger social and supernatural forces, but humans who live within the immanent frame think of themselves as disembedded from cosmic forces and acting as rational, autonomous agents.[19] Rather than conceiving of ourselves as living in a cosmic and hierarchical great chain of being, we conceive of ourselves as living in a flattened universe where the primary goal of human society is to promote individual welfare.[20]

The secular emphasis on individual human flourishing may help to explain our culture's deep suspicion of religious voices. For those inhabitants of the immanent frame who think that God may have purposes for the world beyond that of individual welfare and human flourishing (for example, the transformation of the world, or the glorification of the divine), there is significant pressure to express those thoughts only in private. As Joustra and Wilkinson remark, "To drag this higher command into the public square or the political arena would risk instability, and possibly even repress human flourishing—especially since your individual conception of what glorifies God might differ from mine."[21] Since the work of prophets

---

16. Brueggemann, *Prophetic Imagination*, xi.

17. Taylor, *Secular Age*, 18–20. A helpful introduction to Taylor's massive tome can be found in Joustra and Wilkinson, *How to Survive the Apocalypse*, 10–33.

18. Taylor, *Secular Age*, 505–35.

19. Taylor, *Secular Age*, 221–69.

20. Taylor, *Secular Age*, 505–35.

21. Joustra and Wilkinson, *How to Survive the Apocalypse*, 21.

gives public expression to an alternative way of being, they could potentially give voice to ideas that contradict our secular commitment to the individual pursuit of spirituality or, worse, advocate ideas that are harmful to individuals or groups.

At the same time, the experience of the immanent frame necessitates prophets. Sociologist Ruth Braunstein points out that life within the immanent frame finds many ways to pull our eyes downward and turn our thoughts inward, keeping us from an authentically and intentionally lived connection with the transcendent.[22] There are two significant dangers of the secular age; one is a rampant individualism that leaves us feeling disconnected and self-absorbed. The other is a spiritual and social myopia that narrows our field of vision about what is good and focuses our attention on short term, anthropocentric goods. Myopia is constituted by a lack of imagination for how the world could be, as well as lack of attention to the larger issues that threaten our future. In that cultural condition, the prophetic imagination plays an important role. Prophets, Braunstein writes,

> seek to draw our eyes upward and outward, to inspire us to imagine a world *beyond* our own experiences, *beyond* human flourishing, *beyond* "this life." This can result in a deeper spiritual life, but it can also impact our social lives insofar as it encourages individuals to imagine themselves as interconnected.[23]

Prophetic figures are not confined to the private religious sphere. Perhaps because their vision encompasses the various parts of life that we would otherwise compartmentalize, they straddle the divide between the religious and the political and meet us in the civic sphere. Utilizing tools from both spheres, civic prophets have the ability to envision a transcendent, alternative reality and help us comprehend purposes beyond one's self-interested goals. At the same time, this prophetic vision has the power to knit modern, highly individualized humans together in everyday life.[24]

Despite the myopia and individualism that threaten us, Taylor reminds us that the secular age has brought many benefits. Some of the positive outcomes of our secular age are its growing interest in human and gender equality, its embrace of diversity, and its development of individual rights. If the prophetic imagination requires us to jettison these benefits, then it

---

22. Braunstein, "Political Myopia."

23. Braunstein, "Political Myopia," para. 3. Italics original.

24. Braunstein explores the particular ways in which this happens in her book *Prophets and Patriots*.

cannot speak to the social evils that the secular conscience has brought to our awareness. But if the prophetic imagination cannot challenge our myopic distraction and self-absorption, then it remains captive to the most reductive and corrosive elements of the immanent frame. Taylor's diagnosis thus prompts a re-visiting of the biblical prophets, whose words and lives have shaped the American prophetic experience. On the one hand, it is necessary to grapple with the narrowness of our cultural readings, which focus on the confrontational speech of men who are depicted as operating outside of social institutions and community. Such readings overlook the rich complexity of prophetic men *and* women who are propelled by their relationships with the transcendent god of Israel and by their communities to engage in a host of activities.[25] On the other hand, it is also necessary to grapple with these texts in the light of the benefits as well as the challenges of our secular context.

Prophetic Vision and Voice in Nurturing an Alternative Community

Moses is the prophet *par excellence* in the Bible and in American political and religious culture. From the beginning of Exodus to the final chapter of Deuteronomy, Moses dominates the Torah. Michael Walzer has pointed out that political activists have repeatedly returned to the story of Moses because, "Within the sacred history of the Exodus, they discovered a vivid and realistic secular history that helped them to understand their own political activity."[26] The Exodus story and the figure of Moses have allowed prophetic language and prophetic personalities to thrive within American culture, even during this secular age. As Walzer argues, the story invites secular readings without excluding religious ones.

Americans read Moses as the paradigmatic revolutionary leader who appears to model the prophet as one that "speaks truth to power."[27] Americans have long focused on the Moses who valiantly stood up to Egyptian oppression, went head-to-head with Pharaoh, and assumed the role of the revolutionary leader. As a liberator of an oppressed and enslaved people, Moses's story provided the narrative framework by which our earliest

25. See, for example, Kelle, "Phenomenon of Israelite Prophecy," 275–320.
26. Walzer, *Exodus and Revolution*, x.
27. As Walzer so powerfully demonstrated in *Exodus and Revolution*, but Brueggemann challenges this assumption about prophecy in *Inscribing the Text*, 10–11.

national leaders and our civic prophets understood their own religious and political work.[28] But Moses's biography reveals that he is far from a lone voice or an isolate. Although Americans read Exodus as the story of Moses's clash with Pharaoh, his prophetic career is inextricably tied to that of Miriam, his sister, and also to the exodus community.

Wilda Gafney argues that biblical texts provide two broad categories for prophetic activity: performance and proclamation.[29] Some prophets are distinguished by doing public acts—such as miracles, singing, inquiring of God, and interpreting divine messages—while other prophets mediate the divine message by being persuasive orators and preachers. Moses belonged to the first category. By his own admission, he was not a skilled speaker (Exod 4:10), and when he did engage in extensive orations, it was to reiterate the Sinai Covenant laws—hardly soaring rhetoric.

In his first confrontations with injustice, Moses actually does not speak much at all. In fact, it is his sight that proves to be more important in initiating his prophetic career than his voice. Exodus 2:10-17 says that Moses, having been adopted by Egyptian royalty after his infancy, went out and "saw [the Hebrews'] forced labor" and "saw an Egyptian beating a Hebrew." Witnessing these scenes of oppression seems to have triggered Moses's empathy. He identified with the one who was beaten, and saw (r-'-h) him as "one of his kinfolk" (v. 11). But despite his empathy and his royal standing, Moses did not publicly speak out to stop the beating. Instead, he resorted to violence, killing the Egyptian and hiding the body in the sand after looking and "seeing (r-'-h) no one" (v. 12). The next day, Moses witnessed two Hebrews fighting. This time, he intervened verbally (v. 13), but was rebuffed because of his violence on the previous day (v. 14). In the next scene, he once again intervened in a conflict on the side of the disadvantaged—this time without words. These three short scenes demonstrate that Moses began his career by seeing and acting privately, not by speaking truth to power.

While Moses displayed a nascent empathy and a concern for justice in those early stories, his motivations lacked deep grounding. In the face of Pharaoh's wrath, he chose to flee and protect himself rather than use his privilege as the adopted son of royalty to pursue liberation for his beleaguered kinfolk. He had settled into a pastoral life, though somewhat uneasily (Exod 2:21-22), when he was confronted by the burning bush. It was

---

28. Prothero, *American Bible*, 18–33.
29. Gafney, *Daughters of Miriam*, 25.

through this visionary encounter that Moses found his prophetic calling. YHWH directed his attention back to the suffering of the people in Egypt (Exod 3:7) and compelled him to publicly take up the cause of liberating the slaves. Despite his earlier action of killing the Egyptian to protect the Hebrew, Moses was not eager to take up the cause, in part because he had "never been eloquent, neither in the past nor even now" (Exod 4:10; see also 6:30). His initial ability to see and be moved by the suffering of others was not yet large enough "to imagine a world *beyond* [his] own experiences."[30] It was his relationship with YHWH, initiated by a visionary encounter with the transcendent, that transformed the reluctant figure into a revolutionary and a liberator.[31]

Moses's short-sightedness grew into a capacious and preternatural vision. At the end of his life, standing at the edge of the Promised Land, he glimpsed a panoramic view of Canaan from the top of Mount Pisgah (Deut 34:1–7). That glimpse emphasized Moses's own extraordinary sight despite his advanced age. Thanks to the work of ideological analyses, we know that Moses's vision of the promised land has had a deeply ambivalent afterlife. In the prophetic speech of early American leader John Winthrop, who was called "the American Moses" by Cotton Mather,[32] the ideal of the promised land stood for an American community that was "knit together" in love. That ideal quickly became a trope for Manifest Destiny and, instead of love, it promoted the dispossession and annihilation of Native Americans and the enslavement of people of color.[33] But MLK sought to redeem this vision of the promised land as a symbol of liberation, inclusion, and justice. In his last sermon, given on what would be the day before his own death, King invoked and reframed Moses's preternatural eyesight:

> I've been to the mountaintop . . . Like anybody, I would like to live a long life. Longevity has its place. But I'm not concerned about that now. I just want to do God's will. And he's allowed me to go up to the mountain. And I've looked over. And I've seen the promised land. I may not get there with you. But I want you to know tonight, that we, as a people, will get to the promised land.[34]

---

30. Braunstein, "Political Myopia."

31. For a discussion of Moses as the original revolutionary, see Walzer, *Exodus and Revelation*, 23–33.

32. Walzer, *Exodus and Revelation*, 82.

33. Prothero, *American Bible*, 18–45; Warrior, "Canaanites, Cowboys, and Indians."

34. King, "I See the Promised Land," para. 37.

The biblical trope of exodus to the promised land informed King's concrete political efforts and also his vision of the beloved community, a society in which black and white people are "tied together in the single garment of destiny, caught in an inescapable network of mutuality."[35] Albert Raboteau remarks that King's vision of America as the promised land was not so different from Winthrop's,[36] but King's soaring rhetoric sought to free the image from its bondage to racist visions of America's destiny.

Those visionary moments at the beginning and end of his prophetic career provided the framework for Moses's most important legacy, the establishment of an alternative community rooted in the covenant laws of Mt. Sinai (Exod 20–24). Walter Brueggeman argues that under the leadership of Moses, "the participants in the Exodus found themselves . . . involved in the intentional formation of a new social community."[37] The Sinai Covenant laws defined the community as a "good neighborhood"[38] and an alternative to the realities of Egypt. While Egypt was the place of injustice and oppression toward the Israelite strangers, the Sinai Covenant demanded that the community do justice for strangers and other vulnerable classes (Exod 22:21; 23:9). Egypt was a place where the Israelites were forced to work relentlessly, but the covenant laws guaranteed a day of rest for all (20:10).[39] Egypt was a place where the Israelites were coerced into serving Pharaoh and his gods, but the covenant community freely agreed to serve Yahweh (Exod 24:3).[40]

In the emergence of this alternative community, the Torah repeatedly shows Moses as tongue-tied and reluctant to speak publicly. But such is not the case with Miriam, who is also identified as a prophet (Exod 15:20) and co-leader of the exodus (Mic 6:4). Although the Torah only preserves small fragments of what appears to have been a larger body of traditions about Miriam,[41] those fragments reveal a prophet who raised her voice at crucial moments in the life of the exodus community. She was not a proclaimer in

---

35. King, *I Have a Dream*, 85. See also Smith and Zepp, "Martin Luther King's Vision of the Beloved Community."

36. Raboteau, quoted in Prothero, *American Bible*, 32.

37. Brueggemann, *Prophetic Imagination*, 7.

38. Miller, *Good Neighborhood*, 55–72.

39. Walzer, *Exodus and Revolution*, 23–27.

40. Walzer, *Exodus and Revolution*, 73–82.

41. Frymer-Kensky, *Reading the Women*, 24–28; Gafney, *Daughters of Miriam*, 76.

the sense of being an orator or preacher, but she used her words and voice effectively in connection with her public actions.

There are three key moments where the Torah preserves Miriam's words and acts. The first of these is when she was a girl, watching over her younger brother on his journey down the Nile (Exod 2:3-10). Miriam courageously stepped forward with a subtly crafted question that moved Pharaoh's daughter to protect the Hebrew baby and re-unite him with his mother (Exod 2:7).[42] Her private collaboration with the Egyptian princess became a saving moment for the infant Moses and the yet-to-be-born Exodus community.[43] In a patriarchal society, the care and protection of children is rarely seen as prophetic work. Because it is typically viewed as women's work, the care of children is simultaneously idealized and undervalued. But recently, some faith-based activist organizations have publicly pointed to the importance of protecting endangered children, citing the Exodus story as foundational. In July 2019, Jewish and Catholic groups combined public prayer with acts of nonviolent civil disobedience in Washington, DC, to draw attention to the immorality of governmental policy that separated immigrant children from their families at the nation's borders. While Catholic nuns, priests, and lay people engaged in protest by publicly praying the rosary in the Capitol Rotunda, Rabbi Arthur Waskow, founder of The Shalom Center and former fellow at the Public Resource Center in Washington, DC, helped lead Jewish protests at the headquarters for Immigration and Customs Enforcement.[44] Waskow, whose ministry has been profoundly shaped by the example of Rabbi Abraham Joshua Heschel, pointed to the prophetic nature of their work by calling on the Exodus story. "Pharaoh's attack on children points toward a repeated tactic of tyrants who have planned genocide: Attack the children first," he said.[45] Their attempt to protect immigrant children was nothing less than a Miriam moment.

In the Hebrew Bible, Miriam's prophetic work surfaced again when the fledgling community emerged from the waters of the Red Sea (Exod 15). Miriam's voice marked the event as she took up the tambourine and led the people in a song celebrating their deliverance (Exod 15:20-22), a song that

---

42. Lapsley, *Whispering the Word*, 77–78.

43. For further discussion of the significance of this story, see Lapsley, *Whispering the Word*, 79.

44. Waskow, "Blocking 'ICE' HQ."

45. Berger, "Cross of Human Bodies," para. 13; "Life-history of Rabbi Arthur Waskow."

Moses sang as well.⁴⁶ The song interpreted the deity's work in delivering the Israelites, describing the events in a fashion that went far beyond the earlier narrative description.⁴⁷ It also served to unite the fledgling community as it pursued an arduous journey toward full liberation.

When Miriam raised her voice for the final time, in Numbers 12, she boldly claimed her prophetic authority in a confrontation, not with powers who opposed the community, but with Moses himself. The matter at hand was fundamentally about the democratization of prophecy. In the previous chapter, Moses had expressed his desire that all members of the community would be gifted with prophetic revelation (Num 11:29). In Numbers 12, that principle was put to the test when Miriam raised concerns about Moses's actions. At that point, the democratizing principle was not upheld and Miriam was punished for the confrontation (Num 12:6-10).⁴⁸ Even so, the Exodus community remained committed to her leadership and refused to continue their journey until she had been re-integrated into their society (Num 12:15).

Not unlike Moses who negotiated with Pharaoh at length to free the people (Exod 5:1-12:32), Miriam collaborated with Pharaoh's daughter, a person of power and privilege, to protect one of the community's infants. And both prophets raised their voices in song to interpret and celebrate the community's experiences. Singing and protecting children are seemingly ordinary tasks, but in extraordinary circumstances these acts reject a status quo that would silence the voices of the oppressed and harm their most vulnerable members.

A similar dynamic is illustrated well in the leadership of civil rights activist Fanny Lou Hamer (1917–77), one of our civic prophets.⁴⁹ While Hamer did use her extraordinary skills as an orator to confront the white supremacist powers of her home state of Mississippi and to lobby for the

---

46. According to the biblical text, she picks up the refrain to the much longer song that Moses is credited with singing in the previous verses. However, there are good indications that the song originally belonged to Miriam and that it was later attributed to the more famous prophet (Exod 15:1-18); see Trible, "Bringing Miriam Out of the Shadows," 18.

47. Gafney refers to this act of singing as interpretive prophecy, *Daughters of Miriam*, 80–84.

48. The presenting problem in Numbers 12 refers to Moses's new wife, but there is debate over the meaning of the cryptic reference. Nevertheless, Miriam's complaint about Moses is in the context of prophetic authority. See further Olson, *Numbers*, 68–72.

49. Raboteau, *American Prophets*.

rights of African Americans and the needs of the poor, her prophetic witness was also evident in the seemingly ordinary task of protecting children: she took in children as a domestic worker on a Mississippi cotton plantation and heroically sought help for her adopted daughter who was denied hospital admission because of racial bias.[50] But her use of song marked her prophetic power in a unique way.[51] Hamer, who frequently invoked the Exodus narratives to interpret the civil rights movement,[52] used song at key moments in her activism. After she and fellow activists were arrested and brutally beaten in jail, she sang to comfort and encourage her bloodied friends who were housed in adjacent cells. She also raised her voice in song to embody the voice of the rural people she represented and to interpret important moments for her audiences.[53] One eyewitness described her singing this way:

> She ... would break out into song at the end of her things, and I'm telling you, you've never heard a room flying [like one] that Fannie Lou Hamer set afire.... She has put her finger on something truly important that all of us had felt but she had said. You heard that all the time. What really gets you is that person somehow concretizes an idea that you had never quite been able to fully form. And she did that in this extraordinary ringing style and then ended up singing "This Little Light of Mine." You never needed to hear anybody else speak again.... I'm convinced she chose that song for a reason ... that she knew that [it] summarized her life.[54]

In the first part of this essay, I noted that common assumptions about prophecy are rooted in what Brueggemann calls a confrontational model and what Walzer might call the prophet as "moral censor."[55] In this conception of prophecy, the lone prophet, assumed to be an outsider, positions himself (for this model almost always assumes that prophets are men) over and against a leader, the government, or society itself and speaks truth to power.[56] They deliver ringing indictments against individual and collective

---

50. Raboteau, *American Prophets*, 167, 169, 186–87.

51. Raboteau, *American Prophets*, 163–93.

52. Raboteau, *American Prophets*, 170–77, 196.

53. Raboteau, *American Prophets*, 188.

54. Congresswoman Eleanor Holmes Norton, quoted in Raboteau, *American Prophets*, 192–93.

55. Walzer, *In God's Shadow*, 78.

56. Brueggemann, *Inscribing the Text*, 10–11.

wrongdoing. In this implicit model, the prophet is affected by neither the support nor the disfavor of anyone other than God. He neither negotiates nor compromises. Sacvan Bercovitch, in his classic work *The American Jeremiad*, argues that this assumption profoundly shaped American prophecy. He demonstrated that American practitioners of the jeremiad modeled themselves according to this perception, and "tended to see themselves as outcasts and isolates, prophets crying in the wilderness."[57] It should be apparent from this reading of Miriam and Moses, however, that the confrontational model of prophecy does not adequately account for their narratives, nor does it fully make sense of the careers of King and Hamer, or the work of Rabbi Waskow and those Catholic activists. On the contrary, their stories yield a picture in which the prophetic voice and prophetic performance is used for a range of purposes: collaboration, negotiation, celebration, interpretation, prayer, and also confrontation. But what makes their work prophetic is their relationship with a transcendent power that granted them a peculiar kind of vision about how their society could and should be. In making known a world beyond this life, these prophets did not just dismantle and deconstruct, they committed themselves to nurturing an alternative community. Far from being loners, these figures were rooted in community.

Prophetic Speech and the Limits of the Jeremiad

The prophets who followed Moses and Miriam in the Hebrew Bible did not enjoy the same abilities or status as the leaders of the Exodus movement. Though the biblical editors worked to show the later prophets as the progeny of Moses, the classical prophets had to rely on their words in ways that Moses did not. Walzer argues:

> They are commonly resisted, disputed, denied their title. And the prophet's title can be vindicated only by his words. Though other tests are proposed . . . the true test is this: by his words—rhetoric, eloquence, poetic power, argumentative skill—shall you know him.[58]

The credibility of the prophets who followed Moses was tied to their ability to speak skillfully. In the American imagination, Jeremiah stands

---

57. Bercovitch, *American Jeremiad*, 180.
58. Walzer, *In God's Shadow*, 74–75.

out because of his similarities to Moses[59] and because of his poetic prowess. His fiery language and strident indictments, which spawned the American jeremiad, have had arguably the greatest impact on American conceptions of prophetic speech.

Jeremiah is unquestionably a conflictual, yet eloquent, truth-teller. As Jeremiah scholar, Carolyn Sharp, says, "Jeremiah is rightfully known as a prophet of doom"[60] and one who engages in "absolutely vicious" rhetoric.[61] Take, for example, this oracle of judgment:

> For scoundrels are found among my people;
> they take over the goods of others.
> Like fowlers they set a trap;
> they catch human beings.
> Like a cage full of birds,
> their houses are full of treachery;
> Therefore they have become great and rich,
> they have grown fat and sleek.
> They know no limits in deeds of wickedness;
> they do not judge with justice
> The cause of the orphan, to make it prosper,
> and they do not defend the rights of the needy.
> Shall I not punish them for these things? Says the Lord.
> (Jer 5:26–29 NRSV)

Jeremiah's prophetic life was spent in the shadow of empire. His use of indictment reflects the realities of Babylonian dominance and the inevitable destruction of Judah. Possibly because of the royal ideology of the time, which claimed a kind of exceptionalism for Jerusalem, the Davidic king would not acknowledge the vulnerability of the small nation in the face of overwhelming Babylonian power. Jeremiah's harsh words confront the denial and foolishness of Judah's leaders (including their court prophets) when he says,

> from prophet to priest,
> everyone deals falsely.
> They have treated the wound of my people carelessly,
> saying, "Peace, peace," when there is no peace. (Jer 6:13c–14).

---

59. Davis, *Biblical Prophecy*, 143.
60. Sharp, *Old Testament Prophets*, 76.
61. Sharp, *Old Testament Prophets*, 74.

His purpose was to urge the Judean leadership to submit to the Babylonians in order to guarantee the survival and the future flourishing of the people: "For surely I know the plans I have for you, says the LORD, plans for your welfare and not for harm, to give you a future with hope" (Jer 29:11).

The jeremiad reflects the paradoxical quality of Jeremiah's language. Invoking Israel's covenantal past, it hurls invective against the audience's wrongdoings in the name of a higher authority. But the speaker understands himself to be a member of that audience, subject to the same indictment. Its purpose is to disrupt a destructive short-sightedness and move the community toward blessing. Kaveny points to the social benefits of this invective by contrasting the functions of prophetic speech with those of civil discourse, which is a form of deliberative speech.[62] Deliberative speech is well-suited for intellectual discussion and policy debates, but is not necessarily helpful when addressing matters of moral urgency. Prophetic speakers traffic in fiery language to convey and create strong emotions—especially anger. The indictment, according to Bercovitch, is supposed to act as a stimulant to cut through communal denial and motivate the audience to act. It does not intend to relegate its audience to damnation; instead, it seeks to reassure the community that they can succeed despite failure.[63] But the jeremiad too often trucks in American exceptionalism as well as a corrosive anger. When this happens, its strident language becomes a tool for entrenching divisions and demonizing the other. In the most abusive forms of prophetic indictment, the speaker no longer sees himself as part of the community he is addressing but places himself over and against the people.[64]

Despite its damaging uses, Kaveny argues that the jeremiad can be rehabilitated. She advocates for what might be called an ethical forensic model of prophetic speech. Kaveny argues that Jeremiah can be helpfully read through the lens of Aristotle's notion of forensic rhetoric. Forensic rhetoric, unlike deliberative rhetoric, focuses on identifying past actions and urging an audience to recognize where it has violated its first principles and communal norms. It relies on pathos and anger but, she argues, it requires ethical deliberation in how it is used. This model is perhaps a

---

62. Kaveny, *Prophecy without Contempt*, 252–310.

63. Bercovitch, *American Jeremiad*, 57; Kaveny, *Prophecy without Contempt*, 177–78.

64. Shulman, *American Prophecy*, 13–20; Kaveny, *Prophecy without Contempt*, 286–307.

variation of the confrontational model because it recognizes the power and moral importance of Jeremiah's indictments but argues that its practitioners should be bound by specific ethical principles in using it.

Kaveny proposes that the most abusive aspects of the jeremiad can be restrained by using Jeremiah's oracles to his fellow Judeans, rather than his oracles against foreign nations (OAN), as a model for prophetic speech.[65] While the OANs unleash verbal violence against people identified as outsiders, Kaveny judges that Jeremiah's domestic indictments provide biblical support for a kind of just war theory of prophetic speech. In this just war theory of speech, the prophetic voice is judged ethical when it is compassionate and humble; addresses a pattern of injustices rather than an isolated problem or individual; when it condemns actions and patterns as a way to offer hope; and when it speaks to a community for the purpose of reconciliation and redemption rather than demonization.[66] These are precisely the marks that distinguish MLK's "I Have a Dream" speech from the destructive jeremiads of Preacher Gary, Jerry Falwell, and other religious cranksters.

Despite Kaveny's plea for the ethical use of the jeremiad, one must wrestle with the reality that even Jeremiah's domestic indictments seem to threaten violence—against the weak and powerful alike.

> But I am full of the wrath of the LORD;
> I am weary of holding it in.
> Pour it out on the children in the street,
> And on the gatherings of young men as well;
> Both the husband and the wife shall be taken,
> The old folk and the very aged. (Jer 6:11)

Jeremiah criticizes the elite for their failure to do justice for the disadvantaged, an indictment that fits well with the egalitarian interests of this secular age. But Jeremiah's oracles also speak of violent punishment for all members of the population, including children and the elderly. This vision of collective culpability and punishment is incompatible with the contemporary concern for the individual and raises the specter of a transcendent power whose thirst for retributive punishment not only suppresses human flourishing but obliterates whole societies.

---

65. Kaveny, *Prophecy without Contempt*, 355–57.
66. Kaveny, *Prophecy without Contempt*, 357, 368–71.

Reframing Jeremiah's Legacy: Truth-Telling in the Interpretive Mode

Without denying the catastrophic and even confrontational nature of Jeremiah's rhetoric, the Hebrew Bible suggests other ways of framing his legacy. Although the book that bears his name presents Jeremiah as a figure who is constantly at odds with those around him,[67] it is instructive to see how the Hebrew scriptures position him within a larger constellation of prophetic voices. In particular, Jeremiah is connected to two other prophetic narratives in ways that are hermeneutically instructive: that of the prophet Huldah (2 Kgs 22:12-20), who was Jeremiah's contemporary, and that involving the reluctant prophet, Jonah, whose narrative was influenced by the book of Jeremiah. Huldah's narrative invites the reader to think of Jeremiah as a prophetic interpreter rather than a moral censor,[68] while Jonah's narrative offers a parody that deflates prophetic anger gone awry.

Although she is not mentioned in the Book of Jeremiah, 2 Kings 22 places Huldah's career at a point early in Jeremiah's prophetic ministry.[69] Both prophets enjoyed a certain level of privilege as a result of the support they received from the same powerful family, the Shaphanides, but Huldah was a professional prophet who worked for the king while Jeremiah's ministry was outside of the court. Shulman points out that those who misuse the jeremiad will often claim marginal status, either unaware of or completely ignoring their privilege. The strategy serves the purpose of allowing the speaker to separate themselves from the majority's failures.[70] Huldah's narrative, however, presents the prophetic voice as one that emerges from a place of relative privilege and uses that positioning to effect change. Gafney speculates that her empowerment was not entirely intended: perhaps the king chose her because he expected her, as a professional prophet and also

---

67. Take, for example, the way the book dramatizes Jeremiah's conflict with the court prophet Hananiah in chaps. 27–29. It is presented as if Jeremiah is a lone figure advocating for submission to Babylon, but Carolyn Sharp, *Old Testament Prophets*, 74–76, argues that there were probably two significant factions in Judah—those advocating for submission to Babylon and those advocating resistance.

68. Davis, *Biblical Prophecy*, 4–6.

69. I do not read Huldah's narrative as a report of actual events, but I take seriously the theological construal of Judah's final years that the writers of 2 Kings 22 are trying to present. In the world constructed *within* the text of the Hebrew Bible, Huldah's career overlaps with the early career of Jeremiah. See further, Frymer-Kensky, *Reading the Women*, 326; Gafney, *Daughters of Miriam*, 94–102; Davis, *Biblical Prophecy*, 5.

70. Shulman, *American Prophecy*, 16–18.

a woman, to tell him what he wanted to hear.[71] But if that was the case, she was not beholden to his expectations and laid claim to her power to speak. Her oracle of judgment did not cater to the exceptionalism that was a hallmark of Davidic politics and other court prophets (see, for example, Jer 5:11–13, 28). Instead, she interpreted the oracle "against the interests" of the privileged, a circle that included the king, the people, and even herself.[72] Nevertheless, she is one of the few "successful" prophets in the Hebrew Bible in so much as she was able to convince the Judean king to change.[73] This point is relevant in so much as it urges us to recognize that prophetic work comes from within the community. It cannot and should not be the work of the disenfranchised alone.

Davis argues that Huldah's narrative offers a model of the prophet as an interpreter. The writer of 2 Kings positions her at the end of the book where she is presented as the last of the prophets in the line of Moses, but also first in the era of Torah interpretation. As a prophetic interpreter, Huldah authenticated the Torah scroll that was brought to her and also spoke of its significance for her own period of time.[74] While she presented a catastrophic interpretation of the Torah, to be sure, she had "the clarity to make the divine word intelligible and compelling" to her audience.[75]

Truth-telling in the interpretive mode, as the Israelite prophets practiced it, used anger and pathos to disrupt domesticated and partisan views of the transcendent. Living in a time that was overshadowed by the trauma of imperial destruction, Huldah and Jeremiah are able to see a reality that is *beyond* human flourishing to say the least. Jeremiah's oracles of national destruction, humiliation, and violence shattered a delusional short-sightedness that believed YHWH would quickly deliver the people (or, more likely, the elite) from the grip of a savagely destructive imperial force. His oracles also conveyed a world that was being uncreated through divine fiat and that would ultimately only be put to rights through divine rebuilding and transformation, not through natural development or evolution. Jeremiah's conception of the divine defies simple characterization: the God of Israel is the destroyer and the creator; the one who punishes and the one who identifies with the suffering of the people; the one who demands justice for

---

71. Gafney, *Daughters of Miriam*, 98–100.
72. Davis, *Biblical Prophecy*, 6.
73. Davis, *Biblical Prophecy*, 4–5.
74. Frymer-Kensky, *Reading the Women*, 326.
75. Davis, *Biblical Prophecy*, 5.

those unfairly afflicted and the one who afflicts all; the one who wounds and the one who heals. The deity disrupted and dismantled Jeremiah's reality, but was also the stabilizing force that supported Jeremiah's attempts to make meaning.[76]

The prophet's visceral rhetoric captures the chaotic experiences of catastrophe using an array of metaphors and perspectives that defy every certainty that humans would otherwise cling to. But this strategy, argues Kathleen O'Connor, creates new ways of understanding the devastation and gives language to the incomprehensible.[77] This in turn allows the community to begin to recover from the trauma. Read in this way, Jeremiah's oracles are not so much announcements of future judgement but acts of interpretation: re-created memories of devastation that recast the people's experience of violence at the hands of God and empire.

Truth-telling in the interpretive mode offers an alternative to the jeremiad. This reframing of Huldah and Jeremiah positions the prophet within the community, subverts exceptionalist agendas, and disrupts a shortsighted frame of reference to introduce a vista that is bigger and certainly more terrifying. But the purpose of painting that catastrophic picture is not for condemnation, for the transcendent reality that shapes the prophet's vista ultimately seeks shalom.

Prophecy in Comic Mode

In the Hebrew Bible, truth-telling in the interpretive mode is most frequently associated with anger and lament, but it can also be associated with comedy. Apparently, the biblical writers recognized the limitations of jeremiadic indictment—its propensity to devolve into scolding, self-righteousness, and even verbal violence—long before it became a concern for modern scholars. Remarkably, the prophetic corpus provides a corrective to prophetic anger with a satire on the prophetic calling in the book of Jonah. The term "crankster" is more than a fair description of the prophet Jonah. He is angry throughout the entire book: angry that God would send him to detestable foreigners to preach because they might repent; angry that the people do repent; and angry that God repents and spares the people. But the book offers an ironic portrayal of this anger which serves to critique the prophetic enterprise itself, especially the preaching of Jeremiah, who

76. Stulman and Kim, *You Are My People*, 9–25.
77. O'Connor, *Pain and Promise*, 47–48.

exulted in the categorical destruction of Israel's enemies (Jer 50–52).[78] Indeed, Jonah appears to be modeled after Jeremiah. He and Jeremiah both receive a divine commission that provokes a strong negative response, and both are commissioned to preach to foreign nations.[79] Moreover, the book of Jonah seems to be an ironic fleshing out of Jer 18:7-8, in which YHWH announces that, "if that nation, concerning which I have spoken, turns from its evil, I will change my mind about the disaster that I intended to bring on it."[80] The language of turning or repenting becomes central to the plot of Jonah in which just about every character, even God, repents—every character except Jonah!

Annette Schellenberg describes Jonah as a collection of meta-prophetic statements that takes particular aim at prophetic exceptionalism and xenophobia.[81] The story undermines and critiques the prophet's certainty about the divine plan to punish a sinful and hated enemy. As Kaveny notes, the book's satire urges any would-be prophet to adopt a position of humility in their indictments, since the book shows that "there is no way to map God's designs securely, comfortably, reliably onto human plans."[82] Moreover, comic irony, which works best when turned against oneself, has the power to defuse tensions and disarm its audience. This creates an audience that is more receptive to critique.

A similar use of comedy garnered the comedians Jon Stewart and Stephen Colbert critical and popular acclaim more than a decade ago and has repeatedly earned each of them the title of truth-teller. Through *The Daily Show* on the Comedy Central channel, the comedians pioneered the ironic form of "Faux News" to critique mainstream media, political policies, and American religion. In particular, Colbert shaped his persona to satirize the self-righteous jeremiadic commentary of Fox News personality Bill O'Reilly. The satire was hugely successful—earning its own spinoff, *The Colbert Report*—not least because Colbert's satire of O'Reilly's Roman Catholic moralism was colored by Colbert's own authentic Catholic identity.[83] Colbert's comedic critique came from the inside. To a lesser extent,

---

78. Blenkinsopp, *History of Prophecy*, 270–73.
79. Sharp, *Old Testament Prophets*, 92; Schellenberg, "Anti-Prophet," 354, 359, 367.
80. Blenkinsopp, *History of Prophecy*, 272; Schellenberg, "Anti-Prophet," 359.
81. Schellenberg, "Anti-Prophet," 370.
82. Kaveny, *Prophecy without Contempt*, 405.
83. Oppenheimer, "Jon Stewart, Religion Teacher Extraordinaire."

Stewart played off his own religious background as a secular member of Judaism.

But it is clear that there was more to *The Daily Show*'s comedy than just a cheap laugh at the expense of religion. While the show was intended to be satire, it also proved to be an excellent source of news information. The Pew Research Forum argued that *The Daily Show* functioned similarly to serious journalism by providing accurate information and moving viewers to think critically about political and religious issues that impacted public life.[84]

Mark Oppenheimer, *New York Times* religion columnist, titled Stewart a "Religious Teacher Extraordinaire" because his comedy did not just lampoon religion but also moved audiences beyond their own dogmas to engage the subject of religion with considerable nuance. Stewart accomplished this by taking aim at "the culture of certainty"[85]—not unlike the kind of certainty that the biblical narrator exposes and undermines in the book of Jonah. Kaveny similarly praised Stewart and Colbert for providing a check on prophetic indictment run amok. She points out that, "Poking fun at self-proclaimed prophets delegitimizes their assertions of their own moral insight and deflates the status of the issues they propose as fundamental."[86] Nevertheless, she asserts that comedic irony is not enough. It provides restraint but it does not demonstrate real value as prophetic speech unless it can move the public toward a morally deliberative process. Stewart himself has not been willing to claim the title of prophet. When Jim Wallis suggested—during an interview for *Sojourners Magazine*—that the comedian was indeed a prophet, Stewart demurred.[87]

It is perhaps a reflection on the prophetic character of Stewart's work that since retiring from *The Daily Show* he has been working as an activist for September 11th first responders. On June 11, 2019, Stewart appeared before the United States Congress to issue a challenge to the House of Representatives to continue to fund a healthcare program that supports first responders, many of whom developed cancer as a result of their work at ground zero.[88] The House had not taken action to reauthorize the fund and

---

84. "Journalism, Satire, or Just Laughs? 'The Daily Show with Jon Stewart' Examined."
85. Oppenheimer, "Religion Teacher Extraordinaire," para. 4.
86. Kaveny, *Prophecy without Contempt*, 422.
87. Wallis, "Interview with Jon Stewart."
88. Carter, "Jon Stewart Blasts Lawmakers"; Stewart, "Statement to the House Judiciary Committee."

there had been threats to make catastrophic cuts to the benefits it provided. Stewart's ten-minute speech followed the general contours of a jeremiad as described by Bercovitch. His indictment articulated the standards by which Congress should treat the nation's public servants, and then proceeded to identify the gross failures of the House to live up to standards worthy of a great nation. While Stewart's reference to a great nation could easily have opened the door for exceptionalism, he precludes this possibility by invoking the catastrophic past. Stewart connected America's greatness to the servanthood of the first responders in a time of national tragedy. Finally, he prescribed the means by which the failure could be rectified, and some of America's higher principles—"courage, grace, tenacity, and humility"—might be restored. The rhetoric was fiery and impassioned, but most importantly, it identified a failure that virtually everyone could agree was a breach of the country's covenant with its first responders. In short, Stewart's tour-de-force functioned exactly the way a jeremiad is supposed to work. The next day, the bill was approved by the House subcommittee. Within six weeks, it had received bi-partisan re-authorization from both houses of congress.[89]

Conclusion

Contrary to my students' intuitions, prophetic activity abounds in America, but its character is contested. This is due, in no small part, to the dynamics of our secular age which provokes our suspicion about those who would challenge our flattened universe. This is because our common intuitions of a prophet rest on a hopelessly romantic image of a holy troublemaker; someone who is almost always male, angry, and free of the influences of community. He is a marginal, misunderstood figure whose righteousness is never compromised by the grubby realities of mundane life. Such an image is a caricature at best. Perhaps there are prophetic figures who match this description, but more often they are probably cranks. This image is derived by focusing on prophetic indictments in isolation from the biographies and narratives that account for the person of the prophet. Prophetic figures from Moses to MLK to Fannie Lou Hamer and Huldah spoke from a place of deep, often conflicted, entanglement with their communities. Moreover, biblical and contemporary civic prophets can and do emerge from places of social and economic privilege.

89. Kim, "Senate Just Extended the September 11 Victim Compensation Fund."

In an effort to move beyond a simple confrontational model of prophecy, this essay has focused primarily on the narratives of the prophets rather than on their oracular activity. Gafney's categorization of prophets as performers and proclaimers cues us to the reality that prophetic work involves more than just speech. Biblical narratives reveal almost as much, if not more, about the character of prophetic work than the oracles uttered by the prophets. While the exodus stories have shaped in us a recognition that the prophet is a leading voice in the fight for racial, social, and economic justice, the biblical stories provide a more expansive conception. They allow us to consider whether seemingly ordinary activities that have often been discounted as "women's work," such as the protection and care of endangered children, might be prophetic.

As proclaimers, biblical prophets did use their words to indict and accuse, and this remains the most identifiable form of prophetic activity today. The jeremiad is quintessentially confrontational but one that has become so corroded that it rarely accomplishes what it intends. While Shulman argues that it continues to be meaningful in combating white supremacy, the abusive character of Jeremiah's legacy calls for reframing. Thus, an interpretative model of prophecy offers us an alternative way to think about Jeremiah's chaotic and violent imagery as interpretation rather than confrontation. This interpretive work is profoundly artful, using the imagination to give expression and meaning to experiences that defy simple language. Finally, Jonah's narrative offers a variation of this interpretive work by critiquing and defusing prophetic confrontation through comic irony. Indeed, the career of Jon Stewart suggests that comedic truth-telling and the jeremiad are not just opposite sides of the same coin but can have a mutually beneficial relationship.

2

Civil Religion and Prophecy Revisited

GEORGE SHULMAN

Introduction

IT IS BOTH DISTURBING and instructive to recall how recently scholars of civil religion and prophecy, myself included, were debating Barack Obama's campaign and presidency. That debate was initiated by his founding repudiation of Jeremiah Wright, paired with his claim to represent a "Joshua" moment in civil rights era history; that debate focused on accounts of "prophecy," in relation to his invocation of the mythos of an exceptional civic nationalism, and to his political pragmatism as the elected leader of a racist and imperial nation. Since then, however, Donald Trump based his campaign and presidency on repudiating Obama's legacy, including his invocations of the progressive universalism in the liberal nationalism that has legitimated both American empire and social reform. But also, a powerful "resistance" is now debating how to narrate—to explain and make meaningful—both the event of Donald Trump and the meaning (the legacy and future) of that universalism, as part of organizing and legitimating opposition. In the context of the Trump event, therefore, this essay revisits and as it were updates debates about prophecy and civil religion in American politics.

Foundational Debates about "Civil Religion"

One stream of scholarship about American politics has involved the idea of "civil religion," and so debate about cultural consensus and liberal nationalism. The backdrop was Louis Hartz's 1955 *The Liberal Tradition in America*, which depicted the absolute hegemony of a Lockean liberalism invested in formal rights, property ownership, individualism, and a narrowly procedural constitutionalism. This ideology and regime, Hartz argued, could not grasp structural inequality, make sense of social revolution, or constructively engage decolonization across the globe. For Hartz, McCarthy's paranoid anti-communism was the symptom of this "monomaniacal" liberalism because it imagined even European social democracy as a despotic threat to "liberty." In contrast, in 1967 Robert Bellah wrote a seminal essay that invoked Alexis de Tocqueville's *Democracy in America* to depict a Judeo-Christian "civil religion" as the consensual, but critical and political supplement to an acquisitive liberalism that cannot otherwise articulate collective purpose or "substantive vision."[1]

For the Durkheimian Bellah, "religion" gives the social cohesion and moral purpose without which a merely self-interested and fragmenting liberalism could never have survived. He called religion "civil" because, following Tocqueville, he saw it as the basis of, and yet set apart from, explicitly political and republican institutions that it at once justified and limited. A "civil religion" comprised of moral norms and civic obligations, he argued, was crucial to chasten the idea of limitless freedom derived from myths of the frontier and endless economic growth. More than a hundred years after Tocqueville, however, Bellah called civil religion a "broken shell" because it had consistently been used to justify imperial expansion, racial domination, and an acquisitive, "materialistic" culture. Still, his subsequent jeremiad, *The Broken Covenant* (1975) insisted that civil religion remained a resource by which to justify dissenting social movements, domestic reform in the name of equality, and criticism of both nationalism and imperialism.

At moments of crisis, he argued, political leaders like Lincoln used its biblical language to call a special nation to face both its sins and its higher redemptive purpose; invoking William Lloyd Garrison and Eugene Debs, he argued to sixties activists that critics of racism or empire must speak in widely resonant (biblical) terms, or incur cultural marginality and political impotence. In the American case, indeed, rhetorically effective dissent

---

1. Bellah, "Civil Religion in America."

must take the "prophetic" form of calling people to (re)turn to their own professed first principles and highest aspirations. Critics who do not invoke "any genuinely American pattern of values," the "better instincts of American patriotism" or "the deeper moral instincts of Americans" will fail, thereby allowing a corporate, imperial regime to "undermine essential American values and constitutional order." For Bellah, then, the risk in democratic politics is not faith, what John Rawls called "comprehensive doctrine," but giving up (or ceding to the right) the civil religion that could give dissent a culturally legible, legitimating ground. Paradoxically, then, an effective democratic (or in European terms social democratic) politics must not cede idioms of religion and nationality to the right.

In turn, the "liberal-communitarian" debates were initiated by his own *Habits of the Heart* (1985) and climaxed with Michael Sandel's *Democracy's Discontent* (1998), which challenged the "liberal" vision of an "unencumbered" self, as it were fully formed, rational, and self-interested, entering into social contracts for limited ends. Theories premised on such "liberal individualism," he argued, exemplified in dominant constitutional jurisprudence as well as the political theory of John Rawls, depicts a sociological impossibility, and invests "self-making" liberal subjects in disavowal of their own cultural, social, and material conditions of possibility. The acknowledgments voiced by civil religion are essential to "remind," as Tocqueville put it, possessive individuals (and "factions" deploying the Madisonian machinery of government) of the collective—at once sociological and ethical—premises on which democracy depends.

A powerful critique of these arguments was fashioned by Sacvan Bercovitch. Rejecting the premise that "liberal" and "communitarian" positions were contradictory, he instead depicted how communitarian concerns were in fact internal to a liberal nationalism that showed a remarkable capacity to absorb and disarm dissent. In his view, that is, civil religion authorized, not limited, both liberal individualism and nationalist religiosity. His specific claim was that American civil religion included "the ritual form" of a "jeremiad"—a narrative of decline and crisis, seeking renewal and redemption—that has worked to "contain" voices and movements of dissent in nationalist and liberal terms. Whereas Bellah feared marginality if critics do not use civil religion as a democratic resource, Bercovitch depicted incorporation: a "prophetic civic identity" binds critics to the hegemonic form of liberal nationalism. Whereas Bellah wrote a jeremiad to argue that civil religion could be used to contest the abstract formalism of liberal principles, the exclusions they have justified, and the "arrogance" of an imperial nationalism, for Bercovitch this very genre of criticism works *only* as a "rite of assent." Jeremiadic rhetoric makes "the very exposure of social flaws" into a "ritual of socialization," because dissent is taken as essentially "American," to re-affirm the redemption of an exceptional American possibility. The "dream that inspires [critics] to defy the false Americanism of their time," he thus argued, is what compels them "to speak their defiance as keepers of the dream."[2]

As the jeremiadic form always authorizes criticism by invoking sacred origins and first principles of a chosen people, so criticism in the United States repeatedly confirms the hegemony both of *liberal* principles and of a specifically *national* frame for politics. To refuse either, he claimed, is to sacrifice legitimacy. Distinguishing Eugene Debs from Emma Goldman, and Martin Luther King from Malcolm X, Bercovitch identified the hegemonic gravity defining how critics "must" speak to be legitimate. Contingent yet intractable, this must signals strategic and internal pressures that drive critics to redeem the society they criticize. Accordingly, he argued, American politics unfolds not in conflict over "moral and social alternatives" to liberal nationalism, but through competing calls for "cultural revitalization" of its authentic but jeopardized values. "Civil religion" thus promises that an imperiled people can be redeemed by making good on, not contesting, its founding ideals, which sustains the founding dream of a special nation capable of endless progress.

Grasping how politics in the United States "contains" actors and alternatives because credibility depends on investing "America" with sacred and redemptive meaning, Bercovitch depicted a "poly-ethnic, multi-racial, openly materialistic, self-consciously individualistic people knit together in the bonds of myth," a "modern nation living in a dream," a "collective fantasy" that collapses the secular and the sacred. In contrast, he proposed recognizing the United States "for what it is, not a beacon to mankind as Winthrop proclaimed . . . not even a covenanted people robbed by un-American predators of their sacred trust," but "one more profane nation in the wilderness of the world." What would it mean, he asked, if "America" were severed from "the United States?" The question jolts to a degree that signals the hegemonic grip, unsaid and invisible, that he names, and contests.

---

2. Bercovitch, *American Jeremiad* and *Rites of Assent*.

Arguments about the relation of religion to both liberalism and nationalism have been restaged repeatedly since the new right organized a defensive nationalism that mobilized evangelicals, anti-state animus, and militarization while demonizing 60s dissent and its concern with racial injustice, imperialism, and corporate power. The post-60s academic and cultural left could be said to have reiterated Bercovitch by refusing both liberal language and a national(ist) frame for imagining and conducting politics, while Richard Rorty's *Achieving America*, in 1998, could be said to have reiterated Bellah by lamenting left marginality and defending a "progressive" nationalism in the spirit of Whitman, Lincoln, and Dewey. These debates were sustained during the years of Clinton's presidency, which sought legitimacy and electoral success by accepting the terms set by the "Reagan Revolution;" then again in response to 9/11; and more recently at key moments in Obama's political trajectory. But Obama's political career made visible a second stream of scholarly argument, which contrasts rather than fuses "prophetic" language and "biblical" civil religion.

Defining "Prophecy"

Whereas Bellah and Bercovitch aligned prophecy and civil religion, a variety of scholars have depicted a more agonal or conflicted relationship through accounts of abolitionism, the historic idiom of the Black church, and a radical reading of Martin Luther King. The implication of their arguments is that Bercovitch in fact imposed the very homogeneity he claimed to oppose: because he ignored racial domination and division, he also occluded the radical impact of the ways that critics of white supremacy inflected "prophetic" speech. Indeed, as Black and white critics and activists used the genre of prophecy to contest white supremacy, I myself have argued, they developed a critical view of the liberal axioms, jeremiadic rhetoric, and national frame that have indeed dominated American politics as a "civil religion." Whereas Bercovitch split an incorporated inside from a radical and "un-American" outside, critics of white supremacy—like Frederick Douglass and Henry Thoreau, the radicalized Martin Luther King and James Baldwin—used prophetic idioms to advance an agonistic politics. As they tried to redeem a *democratic* promise from betrayal and failure, they articulated a conflicted and critical relationship to both liberalism and nationalism.[3]

3. Shulman, *American Prophecy*.

Indeed, because they were working not within a democratic framework, but confronting the racial state of exception that at once founds and violates it, these critics also lived a vexed relationship to the democratic ideals they valued. They had to stand in tension with individual rights and not only property rights, with majority rule and the rule of law, with conventional forms of pluralism, customary practices of localism, and ideologies of individual and ethnic mobility, all of which protected slavery, then legal apartheid, and now, ongoing forms of institutionalized racism. We hear this obviously non-liberal form of prophecy when Martin Luther King turns from the problem of Jim Crow to capitalism and poverty, militarism and imperialism. We hear him move against and beyond civic nationalism or even civil religion as he denies providential status to the United States and instead identifies it as the greatest purveyor of violence in the world. As Bercovitch argued, these arguments marginalized the living King and divided the civil rights movement, but the murdered King was re-enfolded within American exceptionalism, as if he stood only for liberal principles and wholly within the national frame. In our racial history, an agonistic prophecy emerges as distinct from civil religion but also as legible because of it.

To say "prophecy," therefore, is to designate not so much the literal words of "The Book of Revelation" as a biblical *genre*, involving characteristic tropes and figures of speech, that is taken up and transformed, from the English Revolution to the abolitionist and black church tradition in America. What is sanitized in a now-canonized King is the radical and political character of the re-workings of this genre by critics of white supremacy. Such reworking may intersect with the jeremiadic narrative of civil religion, and its idioms are readily recognizable even by Americans who are secular, but it entails a profoundly agonist rather than consensual politics. It may intersect with the language of liberal rights as it objects to disenfranchisement, exclusion, and violence in the name of egalitarian respect for the dignity of every human being, and it may register the reality of national identification as it criticizes the already-enfranchised and insists they recognize the membership of people they have disavowed or cast out. But, this prophecy is not oriented toward mere inclusion on given (liberal nationalist) terms, but rather toward fundamental reconstitution of a regime built on domination and idolatry.

Like the biblical prophets, critics in the American prophetic tradition remember what people forget: the haunting consequences of conduct in the past, practices of domination now, and those Toni Morrison calls "the disremembered and unaccounted for." These critics thus perform central aspects of the "office" of prophecy as depicted in the Bible. *First*, they speak as messengers, to announce unspeakable truths and unescapable realities, which people disavow, but which they must acknowledge if they are to flourish. When Amos announces a just god, when Nietzsche announces the death of God, when Frederick Douglass depicts how the freedom of some depends on the slavery of others, when Baldwin names "the price of the ticket," or when Morrison depicts the disavowed past ruling the present, they avowedly draw on prophecy as a genre to make imperative claims about truths we deny at great cost. *Second*, prophecy is the office of witnesses, who make present what has been made absent and who say what they see and stand against it. They bear witness against domination, and on behalf of those who are not counted as real by the enfranchised, but they also bear witness to what our professed principles really mean or entail. *Third*, prophecy is the office of watchmen who would forestall danger by warning of it, and by showing it can be averted if we amend our ways. As we hear when Baldwin warns of "the fire next time," watchmen do not decree a fate, but insist on our capacity to act otherwise, though sometimes they must announce that it is too late to avoid the relentlessly unfolding consequences of past conduct. Their office is not to predict as such, but as Martin Buber argues, to call people to a fundamental and fateful "decision" about constitutive practices and first principles. Thus, if the danger they warn of comes to pass, it means they have failed. *Lastly*, therefore, the prophet's office is to compose songs of lamentation, for they must witness the pathos of our freedom and they must try to redeem the past for the present by endowing our suffering—and self-destruction—with meaning.

In each regard, prophecy is a political "office" because those called to it must address a worldly community about its circumstances and history, its professed principles and prevailing practices, its choices and their fate-ful consequences. Prophecy is also political in the sense that a speech-act conjures into being, to reconstitute, the collective subject prophets ostensibly address. "Prophecy" thus refers not only to an office whose inhabitants make certain kinds of claims about collective life, but to characteristic speech-acts and registers of voice: the *imperative* voice that announces truths we deny at great cost, that declares the costs of (in)action, and that stipulates the terms of redemption; the claim of *judgment* that insists a practice must be overcome, not tolerated or limited; the demand for *action* that declares "the fierce urgency of the now," as King put it, insisting on "decision" rather than deferral of responsibility.

Obviously, therefore, prophetic speech acts seem—and can be—dangerous to a democratic politics organized by the pluralist axiom that all viewpoints are valid. Because critics of white supremacy work not within a democratic frame, however, but address the exclusions and silences that constituted it, this tension is unavoidable. Indeed, in a liberal society especially, critics of domination turn repeatedly to the genre of prophecy because they need to voice problems and concerns that are occluded by liberal idioms of individual rights, formal equality, procedural fairness, preference aggregation, or interest group bargaining. Addressing domination and disavowal, they seek a language whose intensity and cadences perform what Douglass calls "scorching irony," to provoke self-reflection and to elevate the temperature of the body politic.

Civil Religion and Prophecy in the Obama Moment

To return to interpretations of Obama, Jeremiah Wright belongs in this prophetic tradition, as much as Martin Luther King or Frederick Douglass. When Wright announced from his pulpit that god damns America, when he bore witness on behalf of those (whether Blacks or Palestinians) whose reality remains invisible to the enfranchised, and when he warned of the consequences of a house divided by domination or of imperial hubris, he was speaking in the prophetic mode of Amos and King. His loyalty is not to the state as such, to the exigencies of national interest, or to the nation as an imagined community, but to his god and to his people—defined not ethnically but politically as those cast out by power. He thus lives a divided loyalty fraught with productive tension. When he condemns racism and empire, he speaks as a critic not only of social injustice, but of idolatry as the worship of power and reification of identity, which must be chastened not validated. Such a figure, like King and Baldwin, will address the fate of an American whole by bearing witness to the experience and gifts of its excluded part, and thereby seek the mutual reconstitution of part and whole. But when he addresses his congregation as exiles in Babylon, he also speaks in a prophetic mode, just as his namesake addressed the Hebrews about making a life in exile.

Unlike King, Wright may not have effectively or consistently mediated between the civic or constitutional, and the prophetic; likewise he may not have effectively mediated between the two sorts of appeal characteristic of black prophecy in America, one to a white majority blinded by willful innocence, who call themselves a chosen people in a promised land, and the other to subalterns living as strangers in a strange land. He may be devoted to redeeming, not so much America, as its outcasts. But given Bercovitch's argument about the hegemony of civil religion, we need to credit the value and indeed courage in refusal of American exceptionalism, which allows figures like Wright to question the exclusions entailed by liberalism, and the idolatry entailed by capitalism and nationalism. He thus continued a powerful strand in the tradition of Black prophecy in America, and he spoke it in recognizable registers of an imperative and judging voice seeking decision and action. His example, like William Barber in North Carolina, seem a crucial corrective to the "success gospel" that has captured much of the black church during the long "post-civil rights" era.

To inquire about Obama's relation to "prophecy," therefore, is to explore not only the "content" of *what* he said, but *how* he said it. His distancing himself from Wright—and his use of civil religion—must be read in both regards. Surely, Obama was working with and within the civil religion that Bellah and Bercovitch identified with opposed intentions. He invoked liberal tropes of individualism and mobility as he identified specifically as the child, not of slaves, but of an immigrant who embodies the American dream of self-making. He thereby tried to avoid being consigned to blackness, and so to social fixity, deviance, ethnic particularity, and political marginality, while sacralizing liberal nationalism as embodying the very meaning of freedom. At the same time, however, he also affirmed the collective responsibility that Bellah considered the gift of biblical religion to Anglo-American liberalism. Rather than speak in the "prescribed ritual form" of the jeremiad, depicting decline from or corruption of origins, he narrated a story of "more perfect union" in which the gap between national ideals and actual practices would be closed by incremental reforms.

In his accounts of "more perfect union" Obama joined citizens together in a community committed to foster the flourishing individuality of every member, even as he defended making membership both inclusive and diverse. He thus acknowledged and mediated both the promise of individual freedom and the obligations of civic membership. He also confirmed the normative (moral) structure beneath liberal individuality when he denounced the "irresponsibility" of Wall Street in the banking crisis, but also of black men who fail as fathers. He affirmed the conventional moral axioms that, by distinguishing liberty from license, embed individual rights in norms of responsibility. In turn, he affirmed the essential goodness of inherited American values. In these ways he reaffirmed the consensual faith that indeed seems to join white and blacks despite inverted views of racism and its persistence. In the soaring rhetoric in his victory and inaugural speeches, in his Philadelphia address repudiating Wright, and in his speech honoring Selma protest, Obama depicted the onward march of American "democracy," making the civil rights movement one step in the telos of "our" progress toward "more perfect union." He thus proposed a progressive version of American exceptionalism, which evoked but chastened a nationalism called to serve ethical universalism.

It is just as evident that, as he drew on tropes of civil religion, he distanced himself from its prophetic variant. He invoked King, as a Moses figure, and made marching toward a mountaintop a national narrative of progressive reform, but he never announced god's judgment of a guilty people or demanded that people make fateful choices to overcome social practices long deemed legitimate. He did not speak in the voice of scorching irony, of grievance and righteous indignation, that animates prophetic critics of the American regime. To win election he neither offered a tragic retelling of American nationhood, nor demanded a decision about constitutive but unjust practices; he instead affirmed the redemptive promise of American exceptionalism. Joining immigrant mobility and national celebration to minimize racial division, while making his election the sign of racial progress, his narrative elicited unprecedented electoral support.

Obama demonstrated the possibility that the language of civil religion can be put to progressive use to authorize more inclusive state policies. As Bellah argued to students in 1968, it seemed to ward off marginality, in Obama's case the danger of being reduced to a "black" candidate, that is, merely the representative of a narrowly particular and indeed stigmatized minority. He could claim to stand for the whole because his language joined civic nationalism and the individualistic aspiration of so many, while he personally embodied the dream of more perfect union reconciling every element of a divided nation. Indeed, Obama not only "used" the tropes of civil religion, but himself performed its deepest aspirations in a way that solicited identification with him as a symbol of national possibility. But this consensual politics also meant renouncing partisanship—not only the conflicts and ideologies of the past—represented by "the sixties," the Clintons, and Jeremiah Wright, but also stoked by Republicans now. Obama's "pragmatism," his resistance to "ideology" was the necessary supplement to his poetry of national redemption. His wager was that the language of civil religion would enable a black man to win election, but also authorize pragmatic governing that sought and affirmed dominant terms of legitimation.

It seems totally unjustified, therefore, for Obama's supporters to claim he fulfilled the prophetic project of Martin Luther King. True, Obama could not have been elected without the civil rights movement and the enormous and complex changes it initiated, including the widespread but false presumption that we are now a "post-racial" nation. But he was a consensus politician: he did not admit let alone oppose imperialism but took on war in Afghanistan and intensified drone warfare; he did not challenge capitalism, but saved wall street in ways that provoked incredibly consequential populist rage; he did not condemn pervasive poverty, but talked only about the middle class. He sought to make American power more effective—as if to stave off national decline—by making it morally credible in global public opinion. Rather than embrace non-violence, he was commander-in-chief justifying and deploying the most powerful military in history. He surely was critical of laissez-faire excess, of hubris that forgoes diplomacy, and of conceptions of nationhood openly hostile to difference—and after Trump, these positions and gestures do not seem minor. But Obama never stood with god and the disenfranchised to demand justice, to call down god's judgment on a guilty people, or to demand profound changes in fundamental practices. Rather, his poetry of national redemption served the prose of his pragmatism, and his evocation of defining choices was modulated by tones of moderation, compromise, and forbearance.

Three issues seem important to note here. One is the terms on which Obama's critics on the left have identified his limitations. Some emphasize the grip of "neo-liberalism" on his policies, linked to a "technocratic" methodology and elite orientation. This critique has been justifiably extended to Hillary Clinton, but I am emphasizing his progressive form of civil religion, whose terms of legitimacy entailed a pragmatic incrementalism that promised to overcome partisanship. In retrospect, it seems like the universalism of his political poetry elicited greater hopes than he could satisfy by his actual policies and approach to policy; this discrepancy between his poetry and his prose, so to speak, generated intense attachment and disappointment from progressives and the left, because he appealed to the universalism implicit in the civil religion, but was never able to address the structural contradictions—race, capitalism, and empire—that King came to identify as both its basis and its undoing. In sum, to emphasize only his "neo-liberalism," then, is to miss the sources of his appeal, and his contradictions.[4]

The second issue concerns the premises governing how we judge Obama's relation to civil religion and prophecy. For we could affirm—praise and defend—his distance from prophetic forms of speech as the condition of approaching the world in a truly "political" way—as Hillary later argued to Black Lives Matter activists. We thus could celebrate his gifts as a "prince" in a Machiavellian sense. After all, he built legitimacy for a relatively progressive social policy in a political community that remains profoundly Christian, structurally divided by class, pervasively racist in its social practices and unstated cultural axioms, invested—across class and racial lines—in the "American Dream" of individual mobility and in nationalism. His brilliant political performance enabled him, as a black man, to win the presidency twice in a racially divided nation. His evocation of civil religion, but not prophetic critique, was essential to his electoral success and to any of his successes in implementing a progressive policy agenda.

Indeed, we could intensify the contrast with MLK, by affirming how Obama was supremely "political," a virtuoso performer of the art of the possible. Against the norms of prophecy, we could repeat Lincoln's arguments against the abolitionists: an elected official in a democracy is obliged to recognize multiple authorities: the authority of morality, by which slavery was what Lincoln called "absolute wrong;" but also the authority of the constitution, which legalized slavery in the southern states and included a fugitive slave law; and in addition the authority of majority rule and public opinion in a democracy. Moreover, Lincoln argued, if claims to abstract equal rights, however morally valid, simply ignore the reality of inherited historical circumstance and culture, then such claims entail violent change in the name of the right. The alternative to violence is building consensus for a position, even one that a political leader deems self-evidently right.[5]

It is no wonder that Obama identified with Lincoln, therefore, but it is no wonder, too, that heirs of Frederick Douglass—most obviously Cornel West—drew on traditions of prophecy to press his administration in more

---

4. It is also important to credit that Obama, as a black man, had to avoid any appearance of anger if he wanted to sustain his legitimacy. He felt he could not afford the righteous indignation of Bernie Sanders, let alone the rancor of Donald Trump. (Anger is also an issue in gender terms.)

5. Here we see the tension between Lincoln and Douglass. See Oakes, *Radical and the Republican*.

radical directions, to condemn it for drone violence and deportation, timidity on racial injustice, failure on material inequality. This move—as it were from civic nationalism to prophecy—emerges only by seeking *critical distance* from the nation-state and those it enfranchises, from its normative institutions and their axiomatic assumptions. According to this move, political community needs its prophets and their counter-narratives to contest idolatry, inertia, and willful ignorance—as well as incremental pragmatism. Indeed, as political theorist Jacques Ranciere argued, the truly political moment occurs when "the part that has no part" compels a regime to acknowledge the history and realities, the practices and people it has disavowed, a recognition and coming-to-terms that requires a regime's reconstitution. In just this sense, prophecy is not the antithesis of politics but its very condition of possibility. Such a defense of prophetic critique—of prophetic critique as "political" in a deep and true sense—does not preclude appreciating Obama's extraordinary performance, and the very real gains he enabled by working within (not overtly contesting) the culture's central myths.

Debates about Obama, therefore, posit a relationship between "politics" and "prophecy" that depends on definition in a not trivial sense. Rather than insist on irreducible opposition, it seems important not to split off prophetic voice from the conventional (i.e. electoral and legislative) practice of politics, even its implication in state power and violence. Rather than split off the perspective of prophecy from the virtuosity that faces the exigencies of power, consensus-building, and compromise, let us take up the difficult task of holding them in ongoing tension. As Max Weber argued in "Politics as a Vocation,"

> it is immensely moving when a *mature* man—no matter whether old or young in years—is aware of a responsibility for the consequences of his conduct and really feels such responsibility with heart and soul. He then acts by following an ethic of responsibility and somewhere he reaches the point where he says: "Here I stand; I can do no other" ... In so far as this is true, an ethic of responsibility and an ethic of ultimate ends are not absolute contrasts but rather supplements, which only in unison constitute a genuine man—a man who can have the "calling for politics."[6]

Of course, some claim that Obama sustained just this tension, while here I argue otherwise. He failed to vigorously defend egalitarian principles

---

6. Weber, "Politics as a Vocation," 127.

in ways that credited both a common crisis in political economy and continuing racial disparity, and he failed to mobilize support for open conflict with unrelentingly hostile domestic adversaries. He was not able or willing to link the universalism of civil religion to a critical—prophetic—mobilization on behalf of greater equality, against both increasing economic inequality and racial disparity. Of course, shadows of prophecy appear when he deflates chauvinist nationalism, notes that only the United States has dropped an atomic bomb, registers human fallibility, or credits how interdependence allows individual achievement. Still, a combination of technocratic focus, consensual style and narrative failure allowed the adversaries of equality to advance the divisive narrative that enabled Donald Trump's electoral victory.

To debate the relation of prophecy and politics in the case of Obama thereby leads us to our present moment. Given the enraged and hysterical blowback to his election and his presidency, seething underground and overtly organized, it seems important to ask: does democratic possibility in fact depend on addressing directly—not avoiding, minimizing, or sanitizing—the precarity, anxiety, and ghosts that haunt the American house? How do we assess the progressive iteration of civil religion, and the place of prophecy, after Trump's election?

Civil Religion and Prophecy in the Trump Moment

My concluding reflections are meant to be suggestive, because it is too soon to make any credible claims about the future viability of historic forms of civil religion, and of its prophetic alter-ego. But I can offer some ideas with confidence.

First, there is the matter of context, to explain Donald Trump's electoral victory. On the one hand, it seems clear that Obama's technocratic (neo)liberalism did not address ongoing wage stagnation and increased precarity wrought by thirty years of globalization, which crystallized as a crisis in 2008 and the depression thereafter. On the other hand, the cultural fallout from massive migration (since the quota system was abandoned in 1965) was crystallized by the election of a black man, and renewed and intensified the defensive, angry identity politics of whites perceiving economic and cultural displacement. Unlike any other Republican primary candidate, Donald Trump capitalized on the failure of elites, repeated disappointment in the Democratic Party, anxiety about livelihood and the future, and racial rancor. He exploited the wide gap between conventional political language, and pervasive perception of elite disconnection—a gap that also diminished turnout for Hillary Clinton. Across the globe that gap has allowed racialized nationalisms—mistakenly called populist by the media—to emerge. While it is true that Hillary Clinton won the popular vote, and that voter suppression made a difference, I would emphasize a crisis in political language, and a disconnect between political elites and pervasive experiences of precarity, as crucial enabling conditions for Trump's electoral success. At the same time, it is also crucial to see that in American history, experiences of precarity and anxiety about the future among whites have been organized repeatedly by racial tropes and demonizing aliens. The challenge in grasping our moment, therefore, is mediating between increasing inequality among whites and disparity across the color line as underlying circumstance, but also mediating between the ways that Trump embodies both unprecedented changes *and* recurring historical patterns.

In this context, second, what is the current cultural status of historic forms of civil religion? It seems that Trump rejects its key tropes. He does speak a jeremiad of national decline, a recurring narrative in our history. In the name of restoring lost "greatness" it offered an "America First" politics equating national survival with the defense of whiteness and economic potency against demonized aliens, parasitic allies, and corrupt elites. His rhetoric abandons the universalistic "creed" that Obama evoked, and that historically has authorized American nationalism. Trump does not promise to lead the world (by multi-lateral alliances and "open door" trade policies) in ways that secure our own interests but instead depicts zero-sum conflicts in which there are neither steady allies nor widely shared (albeit unequal) benefits. He also rejects the universalist language of civil religion, which has justified but contained social reform in liberal terms, so that incremental inclusion seemed possible and no break with the past seemed necessary. Trump does not "expand his base" by universalizing rhetoric, say by drawing immigrant generations to conservative views of upward mobility and "family values," like the younger George Bush. Instead he mobilizes whites against immigration, demonizes political adversaries, and supports voter suppression to overcome a limited demographic base. He thus repudiates not only the narrative form and redemptive promise in civil religion, but the historic "norms" it authorized, whether civility across party lines, professions of respect for the rule of law, deference to established institutions, and appearances of commitment to racial impartiality.

Trump rejects the most important legitimating tropes and norms of civil religion—creedal faith in the universality embodied by a city on a hill, in the rule of impartial law, in the fundamental fairness of representative government, the innocence of American power, and the abiding goodness of the American people. As Bercovitch argued, American jeremiads typically narrate crisis or decline in ways that produce reaffirmation of this faith, but Trump instead embodies a wholly transactional politics of narrowly self-interested deal-making. If we say that American elites never actually operated by the creedal faith they professed, we approach the idea that Trump is able to reject or ignore it precisely because of pervasive cynicism and rage, that is, because of (a sense of) its *hollowness*. He embodies that rage and cynicism; he performs "the ugly truth" hidden by the pretenses that have always secured elite interests. Indeed, the shock, horror, and judgment of established media serve his persona, validate the very transgressions that authorized his rule and give pleasure to his base.

Accordingly, Trump *can* reject civil religion because it has entered a time of crisis, precisely during the presidency of a figure who masterfully preformed its poetry, but in the context of permanent war, economic decline, and racialized anxiety.

A variety of theorists depict this crisis. Wendy Brown depicts how "neo-liberal rationality," which puts every relation and practice in market terms, has eviscerated "liberal democratic" values associated with common membership, public goods, civic life. For Aziz Rana, the creedal faith in the goodness and the effectiveness of American national power has been undone, by endless war in the Middle East, and by thirty years of economic stagnation. For Greg Grandin, the myth of the frontier, which promised endless economic growth and a "limitless" freedom for human creativity, is also in crisis. Whereas this mythos long supported an exceptionalism promising exemption from history and sedimented inequality, the frontier—as a porous threshold and endlessly receding horizon—is replaced by a wall, a walled state.

My own sense is that we have entered a moment in which neo-liberal ideology is greatly weakened in its legitimacy and rhetorical effect; it is no longer the only form of common-sense governing judgment and conduct because it has been rendered visible, explicit, and contestable. It has been inscribed institutionally over the last thirty years, but it is no longer the only legitimating language in politics as forms of the civic, collective, and democratic are being vigorously articulated and defended in energizing, contagious ways, as ordinary people across many demographic lines act publicly, many for the first time. "Public opinion" is up for grabs in a profound way. If announcements of the death of liberal nationalism and civil religion seem premature, we have entered what Gramsci called an "interregnum between old and new gods," rife with "morbid symptoms" but also with emergent possibilities to articulate and materialize. To avoid the existential uncertainty of the moment, people are likely to turn to and revive inherited genres, what Karl Marx called "the resurrection of the dead." While he distinguished between "tragedy" and "farce" because some resurrections productively engaged a historical moment, whereas others were forms of avoidance, he also proposed a "poetry of the future" that would embrace "the new." How, then, is our moment conceptualized and engaged during this highly charged presidential election in which Donald Trump seeks a second term?

One powerfully amplified voice in the Democratic Party and media argues that Trump is merely an anomaly, that we can return to "normal," that is, to liberal nationalist universalism, "the creed" that has defined American exceptionalism. "This is not who we are," they say. This voice denies that Trump's election is a symptom of our historical liberalism, of its genocidal, racist foundations, its ongoing exclusions, and its hollowness. But if Trump is a symptom of that history, how is universalism being reimagined? In what relation to earlier forms of liberal democracy, constitutional government, or welfare state liberalism? What terms (rhetoric or genre) are available or emerging to advance democratic values? What kinds of recoveries and re-workings are modeled and encouraged? How is "the new" appearing?

Candidates (and elites) will propose to renew or regenerate the creedal claims of the civil religion committed to liberal nationalism. It is as if the ordinary or normal insists on itself, as if people cannot help but submit to its demand to make Trump an exception or momentary interruption in the historically progressive trajectory of American nationalism. It is not just Biden who bears and affirms this demand; generational candidates (say Kamala Harris and Corey Booker) remain entirely conventional in undertaking presidential politics disconnected from social movement organizing; candidates of affect (Beto and Mayor Pete) model the affect of civility, as if its hollowness was not rooted in entrenched structures. Only Sanders and Warren openly address social structures of unequal wealth and power. But whereas Sanders tends to thunder denunciation while avoiding complexity,

Warren actually engages details and produces plausible policies. Still, both foreground the interdependence and mutual obligation of citizens, a universalizing *ethic* to mitigate or enlarge the claims of *ethnos*. Neither invokes novelty; both in effect resume a New Deal project—including a "green new deal"—but in FDR's model they use a pervasive sense of crisis to justify unprecedented programs.

No more than Roosevelt, though, do Sanders and Warren speak a "prophetic" language. They condemn injustice in militant, even strident tones, and demand radical, that is, systemic change. But their language of plans and programs, even as a response to systemic injustice, is essentially pragmatist in orientation, prosaic or realist in its genre character; they summon a social movement, but to "fix" what is wrong, and make things right. They do reverse the big government epithet, but on behalf of other axiomatic assumptions about individual rights, jobs, and the good life long associated with the American Dream—going back as it were behind Reagan to Roosevelt (skipping LBJ's divisive "Great Society.") Unlike prophets, they find external targets to blame, and as a result they do not call for people to transform themselves and their constitutive practices; rather, government (tax) policy and regulatory state power will change a political economy ruined by elites.

Don't get me wrong, I totally support these articulations of a social democratic politics to remake the meaning of universalism. But if we think of climate change or abolition, and the systemic and cultural transformations required of us, we get closer to elements of the prophetic voice I would delineate. In genre terms, what would we expect? First, the claim that there is no credible way to return to or resume normality because the ordinary is deranged. Prophets announce that we are undergoing—but disavowing—a radical change in, indeed the end of our world as we have known it. They inhabit multiple temporalities to depict a tragic historical arc, while prefiguring what lies beyond it *if* we "amend our ways." Second, prophets bear witness, standing with the realities and the people whose disavowal has been constitutive of the society they address; if acknowledgment means transformation of ourselves, our relations, our world, so they also bear witness to our capacity to change. They point not only to social injustice premised on disavowing those we depend on, but also to the idolatry—of power and wealth, states and nations—that disavows the limitations and interdependence defining the mortal human estate. Third, we hear warnings that refusal of acknowledgment and failure to change create disaster, even as they ask if accumulating consequences already make their intervention too late—for us. Lastly, their poetry thus dramatizes suffering and models transformation, but also laments the tragedy of self-destruction even as it envisions a futurity beyond it. These claims suggest I am prescribing a formula, but I mean to suggest genre markers by which to notice (let alone judge) the character of the political speech we hear in a moment when uncertainty—also pain, rancor, and urgency—must be metabolized into conditions of possibility.

In the week before the June 2019 primary debates among Democratic candidates, I heard elements of a prophetic voice in a context that signals the openness of this moment, and the potential place of prophecy in it. I am referring to the hearing on reparations held in Congress, and to Ta-Nehisi Coates's "testimony." In response to the classic liberal individualism of Senate Majority Leader Mitch McConnell, who denied any responsibility for slavery he cast as a discrete, past event, Coates bore witness to the disavowed dependence of the American republic—of its literal worldly existence, let alone its prosperity—on exploiting black labor and violently terrorizing black people. Against the dis-embodiment by which liberalism extracts individuals from both society and history, Coates depicted history as a constitutive and ongoing "inheritance," alive and consequential in the present. He thereby embedded the living *in* history, as its *heirs*, albeit positioned differentially, as those disavowed or enfranchised by history thus far. Like Warren, he registered the staggering disparity in wealth between white and black, but as a legacy of ongoing white disavowal of racial domination. But rather than say "I have a plan," he was doing a different kind of work—to acknowledge injustice and harm and to think through what repair requires, what it might mean for whites and blacks and for the nation as a whole.

As a result, Coates articulated in moving language the implicit assumptions animating the programs of Warren and Sanders: "we are citizens, and thus bound to a collective enterprise that extends beyond our individual and personal reach. It would seem ridiculous to dispute invocations of the founders, or the greatest generation, on the basis of a lack of membership in either group," as if the speaker had to be there. Rather, "we recognize our lineage as a generational trust, as inheritance." We inherit what they did; they made the world we inherit and bear in trust, as they did by the conduct we now honor. The "we" here is "citizens" of this specific nation: He does not invoke an ideal nation to live up to, like Lincoln, but like Baldwin, defines the nation as the history of its constitutive relations. He thus rejects what he calls "fair-weather patriotism," but depicts "this nation" as "both its credits and debits. That if Thomas Jefferson matters, so does Sally Hemmings. If D-Day matters, so does Black Wall Street. If Valley Forge matters, so does Fort Pillow." The question is not "whether we will be tied to the somethings of our past, but whether we are courageous enough to be tied to the whole of them."[7]

These passages seem the most truly Baldwinian of anything Coates has written. Whereas he typically does not invoke a common belonging or shared civitas, but only white predation and blacks as prey, here—at a Congressional hearing, in the people's house—he sustains Baldwin's double-voiced tension in relation to the nation, citizenship, and whites. He does not invoke a redemptive narrative in which reparations could ever do justice or remove our original sin. He does not invoke Obama's teleological narrative of progress. Rather, he invokes what Michael Rogin called "negative exceptionalism" by making racial domination and its disavowal the distinctive, decisive, and ongoing element in OUR history. That "our" signals, at once, whites and their "fair-weather" story, the disavowed history of blacks, and their relation (call it the nation) over time. The "our" signals both disparate experiences, but also an inclusive political (not ethnic) identity because no one—black or white—is exempt from the consequences of history, its credits and debits.

That people are embedded in and entwined by history is the key idea that Bellah drew from a civil religion whose awareness of sin and limitation might be a resource by which to contest or chasten the fantasy of limitless freedom in liberal individualism and the frontier myth. For Bellah, the possibility of a progressive nationalism—and a vibrant res publica or civic culture—rest on cultivating and passing on this historical, social, ethical sense. And we can see, therefore, why or how Baldwin and Coates remain legible because of it, even though both are overtly atheist. The language of "inheritance" poses a political risk, because it seems to define action only as reaction, as mere derivation, as if people are defined only by descent, but Baldwin typically paired it with an idea of "birthright" to suggest the creative capacity to initiate what Arendt called natality. If Arendt's version of natality risked abstraction or disembodiment, as if our capacity to begin

---

7. Black Wall Street is the Tulsa pogrom in 1921; in Fort Pillow, Tennessee, in 1864, black Union soldiers were massacred by Confederate troops rather than treated as prisoners of war.

is separated from (the bond with) the mother, Baldwin argued both that human beings are engendered, and that we make use of our past, as if springing from it, but also refusing, overcoming or reworking it as we re-narrate its meaning for us now, in the present.

I take Coates as modeling a political—because prophetic—voice. I hear him reading the Donald Trump event back into American history, to register the ways in which it is symptomatic of truly historic patterns, and of political impasse and culture war since 1968. To offer such epic and tragic narration of history, to impel collective self-reflection, is the vocation of prophecy at this moment. It seems crucial but absent in both political speech and media commentary now. My assumption and my claim is that the grip of this bloody and haunting history, as well as the causes and impact of this Trump event must be narrated and acknowledged if we are to make our current crisis a condition of possibility, of creative action. Coates's public testimony, therefore, is auspicious, indicative of the possibility whose conditions he cultivates by his speech. Likewise, Trump's presidency has not only demoralized people. It has also generated active opposition, for we also see energized politics, pervasive and intense participation as well as contest, a ground-level renewal of democratic ideals and practices, what I would call popular prophecy in action. What Martin Buber argued about biblical prophecy remains pertinent: rather than predict a future, this voice dramatizes and models a capacity for decision in the fierce urgency of the now.

3

The Revolutionary as Prophet

Imagining New Futures, Theorizing "What Could Have Been," and Rejecting the Ways of the World

Roberto Sirvent and Andrea Smith

In his editorial for the special issue of *Comment* magazine, titled "Join the Anti-Revolutionary Party," philosopher of religion and cultural critic James K. A. Smith begins with some frank words: "You have nothing to lose but your hubris."[1] Attacking both liberals and conservatives in the North American context for seeking revolution in people like Bernie Sanders, Donald Trump, and even Canadian Prime Minister Justin Trudeau, Smith concludes that "revolution*ism* is now the ethos of our society." Indeed, he adds, it "is the new status quo." Feeling almost marginalized in the public sphere for not jumping on board the revolution train, Smith observes, "You can barely get a hearing anymore unless you plan to burn everything to the ground."[2]

Smith's goal is to introduce readers to what he calls "the anti-revolutionary posture of the Reformed tradition, and the Christian tradition more broadly." Ibid. Among the many critiques that this "tradition" has for revolution-inclined American Christians, three of them are pertinent to our

---

1. Smith, "Editorial: Join the Anti-Revolutionary Party."
2. Ibid., paras. 3–5. Italics original.

argument below. First, Smith claims that revolutionaries aim to "start over from scratch" and suggests that starting over from scratch is not something that "fallible human beings have the wisdom" to do. "Revolutionaries refuse any inheritance, deny any debts," he writes, "confident that their technocratic enlightenment is just what the world has been waiting for."[3] "Behold," Smith quips sarcastically, "*we* make all things new."[4] Second, and relatedly, Smith argues that revolution requires a certain kind of arrogance. "What sort of hubris," he writes, "does it take to assume that everyone before us had it wrong?" Smith adds that this arrogant idealism is a rejection of eschatological hope and that only by awaiting the *parousia* can Christians be "liberated from revolutionary hubris."[5] Third and finally, Smith claims that revolutionaries naively subscribe to a false choice of seeking either revolution *or* the status quo. Smith, therefore, invites Christians to imagine a "robust vision for *reform* as a wise, strategic, faithful pursuit of justice and the common good."[6] And in an admonition that so perfectly sums up his perception of how revolutionaries view the world, he writes, "There might be ways to effect change that don't require scorched earth, all-or-nothing reengineering of everything that's preceded us."[7]

In this essay, we aim to use James K. A. Smith's editorial as a springboard to tear down a few misconceptions Americans might have about their "revolutionary" counterparts. In other words, we do not aim to provide an extensive analysis of, or close engagement with, Smith's text. Rather, we address his thoughts as merely representative of a larger American suspicion of revolution. Our main argument is that the revolutionary approaches offered by scholars in the fields of American Studies, Indigenous, Black, and Critical Ethnic Studies serve as a prophetic critique to anti-revolutionary manifestos such as Smith's. Thus, it is not just fruitful but *imperative* that religious communities and theologians look to secular academic disciplines for guidance. For this reason, we build on the work of such scholars by articulating prophecy as an imagining of otherwise worlds.[8] As Lindsay Nixon notes, this decolonizing imaginary of otherwise futures counters

---

3. Ibid. paras. 14, 7–8.
4. Ibid. para. 8. Italics original.
5. Ibid. paras. 7, 14.
6. Ibid. para. 9. Italics original.
7. Ibid. para. 9.
8. Nixon, "Visual Cultures of Indigenous Futurisms."

the death imaginary in which people of color and Indigenous peoples are subject to "premature death."⁹

Our essay is divided into three sections. First, we dismiss Smith's claim that all revolutionary struggles aim to "start from scratch." Second, we show that the most promising revolutionary struggles are not grounded in *hubris*, as Smith argues, but *humility*. Third and finally, we reject Smith's premise that robust *reform*, rather than *revolution*, is the path to what he calls the "wise, strategic, faithful pursuit of justice." In the process, we hope to show that the prophetic role of these critical ethnic studies scholars and abolitionists serves as a critique of power, privileging the insights of the oppressed when discerning what true justice looks like. We also embrace these theorists as prophets who reject the "ways of the world"—and therefore reject the ideology and idolatry of secularism—by imagining new futures and new worlds, no matter how fractured they may be.

Starting from Scratch?

This section draws on the works of abolitionists to show how the revolutionary's approach is not to start from *scratch* but to start from *the lived experiences of oppressed communities* in order to imagine—collectively—what a just world might look like. Far from (in the words of Smith) "refusing any inheritance" or "denying any debts," abolitionists draw heavily on their rich traditions to discern what they owe to future generations, their present communities, and to those who came before them. As such, the aim is not, as Smith thinks, to pursue a "scorched earth" policy or to "burn everything to the ground." The revolutionary approach is far more nuanced, sometimes requires a lot more patience, and always holds on to what is *already* true, good, and beautiful. In the words of Fred Moten, the main questions to ask are not just "What do we not have that we need?" or "What do we want or want to get?" The other, perhaps more important question might be, "[W]hat do we have that we want to keep?"¹⁰

It is important that "revolution" is itself a contested topic. And it is always important to remember that if anyone really knew how to end global oppression, we would have done it by now. Thus, a revolution is a process of making the road as we walk, as the saying goes. Revolution is essentially a process rather than a destination that requires constant self and collective

---

9. Nixon, "Visual Cultures of Indigenous Futurisms"; Gilmore, *Golden Gulag*, 28.
10. Harney and Moten, *Undercommons*, 121.

critique, change, adaption and transformation. Because we have all been so structured in the logics of white supremacy, capitalism, settler colonialism, etc., if global oppression were to end tomorrow, no one would even understand where they were. Or as Moten notes, white supremacy is not simply about the belief in white superiority; it structures belief itself. Essentially then, revolution is not simply about a change in political and economic structures, but it's about becoming new people in the process. Or as Frank Wilderson and Alexander Weheliye argue, liberation requires a complete reconceptualization of what we consider the human to be so that it is not, in Sylvia Wynter's words, the overrepresentation of white, western Man.[11]

The challenge, of course, is that we do not have access to what we would be like or what the world would be like if the world was not structured by logics of oppression. There is no "outside" that is pure from oppression from which we can move. Thus, a revolution requires us to build a new world from the tools that we have even as we recreate the world in the process. Many Indigenous thinkers do in fact hold that we *can* see a different possible world, given that indigenous nations were not generally structured by hierarchy and oppression prior to colonization.

But even so, as Frantz Fanon noted in *The Wretched of the Earth*, there is no simple access to the prior of the rupture created in history by the colonial moment. As many Indigenous feminist scholars have noted in particular, colonialism shapes what is remembered about the pre-colonial past.[12] But that does not mean these memories are pointless. Rather, if we know we lived differently in the past, then we know we can live differently in the future. There is nothing natural or inevitable about the world we live in now. And just because there is not an "outside" to the current world order, it does not mean we cannot see glimpses of what another world can be now.

This is why so many women of color organizations in particular do not just focus on organizing against the system but focus on building the world we want to live in now. Through experimentation, trial and error, we no longer have to wait for an endlessly deferred revolutionary future, but we can start living it now.[13] This practice is essential because one of the fears people have of engaging in a revolutionary process is that they can only see what they might lose, and have no idea of what they can gain. By creating

---

11. Weheliye, *Habeas Viscus*, and Wilderson, *Red, White and Black*.

12. See for example, Denetdale, "Chairmen, Presidents, and Princesses," and LaRocque, *When the Other Is Me*.

13. Rojas, "Are the Cops in Our Heads and Our Hearts?"

spaces that begin to mirror the world we would like to live in, people can begin to imagine an otherwise world.

Thus, in one respect, a revolution is starting from scratch because it is creating a world for which we have no vocabulary. But at the same time, it engages us as we are now, and not as idealized revolutionaries we think we should be. It engages us in all our contradictions, complications and problems, knowing that no pure revolutionary subject exists. In addition, a revolutionary future, while new, is not necessarily the opposite of what we have now. Some scholars have critiqued the paradigm of "decolonization" as an extractive process by which one is supposed to eliminate any and all counter-revolutionary tendencies.[14] Similarly, Scott Lyons's *X-Marks* contends that a politics of decolonization has the danger of lapsing into a politics of purity in which any engagement with the current legal and economic system is dismissed as co-opted. "If you happen to live away from your homeland, speak English, practice Christianity, or know more songs by the Dave Matthews Band than by the ancestors, you effectively 'cease to exist' as one of the People."[15] While Lyons does not dismiss the importance of decolonization, he argues that such politics do not begin from an imagined pre-colonial past but under the conditions we currently live. Rather than articulate contemporary Native identity as an "impure" version of traditional identity, Lyons argues that such a framework locks Native identity in the past and cedes the "modern" to whiteness. Decolonization entails not a going backward to a pre-colonial past, but a commitment to building a future for indigenous peoples based on principles of justice and liberation.

However, instead of thinking of the revolutionary future in a reactive way in which everything is the opposite of what we have now, we can see it as being in non-correspondence to what we have. This means that there are elements that we would keep, although perhaps in a different relationality. Kara Keeling suggests that the "outside" should not be seen as the opposite of the current system, but instead imagined as being in non-correspondence to the current order. Thus, since it is not the opposite of our current grid of intelligibility, we may be able to see glimpses of the outside—ghosts that gesture toward a beyond—within the current systems.[16] And, as a result, we do not have to reject everything within the current system in our quest for liberation. Some theoretical concepts within Native studies can help

14. Sailiata, "Decolonization."
15. Lyons, *X-Marks*, 139.
16. Keeling, "Looking for M—."

elucidate her arguments. The work of Vine Deloria Jr. has provided much of the theoretical grounding for Native Studies. He argued that decolonization required a fundamental epistemological shift that questioned the very logic systems of western thought itself. In *God is Red*, he articulated what he viewed as some of the distinctions between western and indigenous thought systems such as the distinction between spatial versus temporal orientations, circular versus linear time, and practice versus belief centered traditions. However, as Scott Lyons notes, these concepts started to become taken very literally such that Native scholars started insisting that Native people "think in circles." However, we think Deloria's analysis could be better understood not as a literal reading of indigenous epistemologies but as a gesture toward beyond the colonial order. Because of colonization, one must articulate these frameworks within colonial terms. Yet, colonialism cannot contain them either. What Keeling suggests, then, is that these gestures toward the beyond are critically important, but we should not mistake the gestures for the "beyond" itself.

It is important to recognize that revolutionary work is messy and uncomfortable. It requires us to, in the words of Dylan Rodriguez, "think the unthinkable, imagine the unimaginable and make the impossible a reality." Because it is a politics based on perpetual uncertainty, there is never a firm ground on which to stand. It is thus not surprising that many people would prefer the comfort of the known to an unknown future. This stance is problematic, however, in that it invisiblizes the millions of people who are dying through hunger, war, torture, environmental racism, and all other structures that subject them to premature death. Their only alternative to an uncertain revolutionary future is no future at all. And at the rate of environmental decline we are currently facing, soon there will be no future for any of us.

Thus, a revolutionary process is indeed risky and should be acknowledged as such. However, by collectivizing the process, conducting it in a transparent, self-critical and egalitarian manner, we are in more of a position to correct our mistakes along the way. This is why so many revolutionary groups understand that the revolution is a process rather than a destination. Because it is a process based on uncertainty, we resist the temptation to typologize or define "revolution" because it is not a "thing." It is by necessity always open to contestation with multivalent meanings. The desire to define "revolution" is to domesticate it. In fact, we could similarly argue that many theological projects which seek to define

Jesus, faith, God, etc. are also domesticating projects that render a God of the impossible to that which is easily knowable and thus ultimately what Antonio Viego would define as a "dead subject."[17] Our project then is less to define and prescribe and more to suggest possibilities beyond what we can easily "know."

Revolutionary Hubris or Humility?

The second main point of contention we have with James Smith's anti-revolutionary manifesto involves his charge that seeking revolution is inherently hubristic. What we will see, however, is that the revolutionary's practices are characterized by a remarkable humility. Contrary to what Smith argues, the best revolutionaries do not believe "that everyone before us had it wrong." In fact, many of them study history primarily as a way to inquire about "what could have been." Ideally, this inquiry leads one to imagine alternative ways of being in *this* world, while gesturing towards other, more just worlds in the future.

Students often wonder why teachers would waste their time talking about the 'failures' of history. What is the point, for example, of learning about failed resistance movements against capitalism or slave revolts that were quickly quenched and later forgotten? Why should scholars dig deep into the archives to recover lost narratives that did not "stand the test of time"? If these ideas were *really* important, one might argue, why weren't they preserved and widely disseminated? If these stories *really* mattered, why have we stopped telling them? In other words, is there not a good reason for why these narratives did not make the history books? Is there not a good reason for why they did not 'win'?

Yet if history's 'failures' should only be studied so we don't repeat the mistakes of the past, then why are so many American Studies scholars committed to studying what has become known as *history from below*? For such historians, studying narratives that were lost or movements that were 'defeated' serves as a way to imagine "what could have been." Peter Linebaugh and Marcus Rediker's *Many-Headed Hydra* offers one important example.[18] Their work shows that as long as there has been capitalism there has been *anti*-capitalism. Yet we do not give it a history. Lisa Lowe, in her book *The Intimacies of Four Continents*, troubles the colonial archives

---

17. Viego, *Dead Subjects*.
18. Linebaugh and Rediker, *Many-Headed Hydra*.

to offer a similar critique of the inevitability of capitalism, as well as to dismantle the linear liberal narrative of freedom overcoming slavery.[19] Finally, Raúl Coronado, in his book *A World Not to Come*, gives us a window into nineteenth-century Latino print culture and intellectual life to provide an alternative history of modernity and the dominant westward expansion narratives we have become so accustomed to.[20]

Theorizing "what could have been" serves as a way for historians to conceive of the past as a way to help us imagine new futures apart from dominant ideologies that have "won out." Lisa Lowe, for example, refers to "[t]he past conditional temporality of 'what could have been'" as symbolizing

> a space of attention that holds at once the positive objects and methods upheld by modern history and social science, as well as the inquiries into connections and convergences rendered unavailable by these methods. It is a space of reckoning that allows us to revisit times of historical contingency and possibility to consider alternatives that may have been *unthought* in those times, and might otherwise remain so now, in order to imagine different futures for what lies ahead. This is not a project of merely telling history differently, but one of returning to the past its gaps, uncertainties, impasses, and elisions; it is tracing those moments of eclipse when obscure, unknown, or unperceived elements are lost, those significant moments in which transformations have begun to take place, but have not yet been inserted into historical time.[21]

Thus, the task of inquiring about "what could have been" is not about presuming to tell history "as it really happened" or even to put together historical pieces of the puzzle in some sort of coherent and intelligible form. Rather, as Raul Coronado argues, histories of those who attempted to produce social imaginaries that were never fully realized "remind us of our own contingencies." "The failures of these becomings," he adds, "remind us of the tenuousness of our own desires to flourish as well." Coronado shows how, at their best, these lost histories "enrich our own imaginaries by reintroducing concepts that had been discarded or, perhaps more accurately, existed only liminally."[22] As María Elena Martínez observes,

19. Lowe, *Intimacies of Four Continents*, and Mann, "Theorizing 'What Could Have Been.'"
20. Coronado, *World Not to Come*.
21. Lowe, *Intimacies of Four Continents*, 175.
22. Coronado, *World Not to Come*, 394–95.

recovering these histories provides an "opportunity to discover in the past human possibilities and imaginings that were suppressed or left unfulfilled but that can provide guidance in the present for creating better worlds in the future."[23]

The practice of imagining "what could have been" is in fact a *prophetic* one. The prophetic aspect of this inquiry, as we have seen, speaks to the past, present, and future. It speaks to the *past* by showing us how dominant structures and ideologies of today were never inevitable; they have always been contested. Because they were never inevitable, our *present* conditions are therefore not permanent.[24] And because they are not permanent, it is possible to imagine and create a different world—a different *future*. By invoking the prophetic language of "what could have been," we wait to see how voices of the past can help us imagine a world without prisons, borders, and capitalism, no matter how impossible it might sound. We are also well aware of the possibility that these dreams might not be realized in our lifetime. At the same, we do not need to presume failure. Christians believe in the God of impossible rather than the God of the possible. To assume failure is inevitable is to place our fears at a higher status of worship than God. Thus, besides their humble engagement with the ignored, forgotten, and elided voices of history, revolutionaries also recognize that the creation of a "new world" is going to involve lots of trial and error along the way.

The Idolatry of Reform

Our third and final section addresses Smith's contention that Americans should focus more on pursuing "robust" reform rather than revolution. The revolutionary is skeptical of such approaches for a number of reasons. To begin with, viewing the system as broken and needing to be fixed (i.e. reform) fundamentally ignores the fact that many of the oppressive structures communities face are *not* in fact broken—they are working *exactly as they are intended*. Whether it is laws, regulatory agencies, the police, or other bureaucratic arms of the state, the problem is *not* that someone like

---

23. Martínez, "Archives, Bodies, and Imagination," 174.

24. Here, we remain sensitive to Calvin Warren's important criticism against "the humanist fantasy (or narcissism) that anything humans have created can be changed. Some creations are no longer in the hands of humans, for they constitute a horizon, or field, upon which human existence itself depends. Antiblackness is such a creation." See Warren, *Ontological Terror*, 24.

a President, lawmaker, or police officer has veered off track by condoning or perpetrating violence against vulnerable populations. Rather, they are conducting business as usual. This is why in the days following the Charlottesville terrorist attack, chants exclaiming, "This isn't who we are" misses the point rather spectacularly. White supremacy is *exactly* who we are. As many cultural theorists and American studies scholars have shown, violence, racial terror, and oppression are *constitutive* of American identity, not a radical departure from it.[25] Or as Dylan Rodriguez says, "Brutality, torture, and excess should be understood as an essential element of American statecraft, not its corruption or deviation."[26]

Legal theorist and activist Dean Spade discusses how these patriotic narratives that ground American law as a kind of neutral, benevolent, and color-blind apparatus has profound effects for how we approach social movements. Among the lies we have been told, he writes,

> is that the United States is a democracy in which law and policy derive from what a majority of people think is best, that the United States used to be racist and sexist but is now fair and neutral thanks to changes in the law, and that if particular groups experience harm, they can appeal to the law for protection. Social movements have challenged this narrative, identifying the United States as a settler colony and a racial project, founded and built through genocide and enslavement.[27]

Focus on reform, then, is merely an attempt to entrust one's liberation into the hands of the oppressor itself. Of course, this is not to say that one cannot simultaneously fight for meaningful reform *and* revolution. Theorists like Mariame Kaba, Dan Berger, and David Stein, for example, stress the importance of fighting for "non-reformist reforms." These reforms, they argue, consist of "measures that reduce the power of an oppressive system while illuminating the system's inability to solve the crises it creates."[28] In other words, non-reformist reformers ensure that those communities currently targeted by state violence are attended to. Yet at the same time, they make sure none of these reforms expand the state's imperial and carceral power. Again, abolitionists reject any notion that the state can be "reformed" from an apparatus that perpetrates violence to one that *protects*

---

25. See for example Hartman, *Scenes of Subjection*.
26. Rodriguez, *Forced Passages*, 47.
27. Spade, *Normal Life*, 2.
28. Berger et al., "What Abolitionists Do," para. 4.

us from it. As Spade writes, reform efforts often ignore "that state programs and law enforcement are not the arbiters of justice, protection, and safety but are instead sponsors and sites of violence."[29]

If George Shulman is right that the role of the prophet is to testify against idolatry,[30] then it is worth examining how the revolutionary's rejection of reform also serves as a rejection of secularism—the idol of binding oneself to the "ways of the world." In his article "Black Religion as Black Radicalism," Vincent Lloyd writes:

> The ways of the world are grotesquely wrong. To see justice prevail on earth, a dramatic transformation of individuals and society would be necessary. Our present habits of thinking, seeing, and acting must be uprooted. These truths are most evident to the most marginalized—in the contemporary United States, to poor blacks—and it is in the struggle of the most marginalized that we catch glimpses of what justice (and beauty, and goodness, and truth) looks like.[31]

Prison abolitionist Eric Stanley connects this prophetic spirit with the imagination required to resist romantic views of reform discussed above. In an interview with *bluestockings magazine*, Stanley speaks about the abolitionist "commitment to dreaming collectively beyond and against the pragmatism of the political as such."[32] Later, he aptly describes abolition as a "pre-figurative" that shows "how the prison system is not 'broken,' as many argue, but it is working exactly as designed; as a set of interlocking practices, laws and fantasies that liquidate entire life-worlds, particularly Black, Native, gender non-conforming, disabled, undocumented and more."[33]

Thus, revolutionaries are not, as James Smith argues, guilty of having limited imaginations which prevent them from seeing beyond the false choice of status quo or revolution. If anything, they dream bigger—much bigger than those who dream of 'robust reform.' They agree with Lloyd's call, not for more pragmatic reasoning in the public sphere, but for an uprooting of the way we think, see, and act. It is the exact point that Fred Moten makes when he asks: "What is, so to speak, the object of abolition?" His answer? "Not so much the abolition of prisons," he writes, "but the

---

29. Spade, *Normal Life*, 2.
30. Shulman, *American Prophecy*, 7.
31. Lloyd, "Black Religion as Black Radicalism," para. 4.
32. Morris, "On Trans and Queer Prison Abolition," para. 4.
33. Morris, "On Trans and Queer Prison Abolition," para. 4.

abolition of a society that could have prisons, that could have slavery, that could have the wage, and therefore not abolition as the elimination of anything but abolition as the founding of a new society."[34]

Whether or not these abolitionists and revolutionaries claim some sort of faith commitment, they all join in rejecting the ideology—and idolatry—of secularism. To borrow from Eric Stanley's quote above, we have become too wedded to "the pragmatism of the political." As Vincent Lloyd observes:

> Secularism is the name for this problem. It does not just mean rejecting or ignoring religion. Secularism means embracing the world as it is given to us (in medieval Europe *saeculum* meant "the world"). It means accepting the choices on the table, a table set by the ruling class. It wants to make healthcare more affordable—not free. It wants to give the police better training, to give soldiers humanitarian missions—not abolish the police and the military. It wants to make slavery, or wage slavery, more comfortable—not bring them to an end.[35]

To most people, these proposals about abolishing prisons, the police, and the military might sound unrealistic, if not downright impossible. But any revolutionary would admit that rejecting the ways of the world requires quite a bit of faith. As Hebrew 11:1 states, "Now faith is, the substance of things hoped for, the evidence of things not seen." Faith requires us to believe in a revolutionary future for which we can not only not see, but not even describe. Whether we describe it as the status quo, the pragmatism of the political, or the choices on the table, refusing the "ways of the world . . . takes faith in things unseen," Lloyd concludes. "Some call it God, some call it revolution—is there a difference?"[36]

Conclusion

In the opening essay of this edited volume, George Shulman argues that prophecy includes a connection between past, present, and future. If he's right, then the field of American Studies is, at its best, a site of prophetic thought. For it reminds us that a true revolutionary is not the one planning "to burn everything into the ground," as James K. A. Smith argues. Rather,

---

34. Harney and Moten, *Undercommons*, 43.
35. Lloyd, "Black Religion as Black Radicalism," para. 11.
36. Lloyd, "Black Religion as Black Radicalism," para. 7.

the revolutionary is a prophet who laments over—and draws inspiration from—"what could have been." By reflecting on these "failed" collective struggles of the past, communities are better equipped to challenge domination in the present and imagine new, just worlds for the future.

4

Wanting Prophecy

Prophetic Storytelling at the End of a Way of Life

John Elia

We stand on the brink. Yet many Americans seem dimly aware of it. In its politically white-washed form we call it "climate change."[1] Some scholars have rebranded it the "Anthropocene," lending, regrettably their critics say, to academic distance more than a worldwide S.O.S. call. Mainstream media has hardly helped: when the Intergovernmental Panel on Climate Change (IPCC) published a special report in fall 2018 arguing that we have twelve years to slash carbon emissions by 45 percent to maintain a 1.5°C (2.7° Fahrenheit) average global temperature increase, only twenty-two of the top fifty newspapers in the United States covered it.[2] An active disinformation campaign by the so-called Merchants of Doubt, who lobby for the fossil fuel industry, has sown confusion and polarization.[3] As I write in the summer of 2019, commentators are urging that the IPCC's twelve-year

---

1. The Trump administration will not stand even for that anodyne term, removing mentions of climate change from agency reports, press releases, and websites, and otherwise burying climate science. Waldman, "Trump Administration Officials Scrubbed."

2. Intergovernmental Panel on Climate Change, "Special Report: Global Warming"; Hertsgaard and Pope, "Media Are Complacent."

3. Hertsgaard and Pope, "Media Are Complacent."

window for climate action could close, politically speaking, in the next twelve to eighteen months.[4]

Climate rhetoric matters. While reason and evidence must be consulted, we need a prophet, or, rather, many, who can name our sins, forecast our futures, and move us to atonement if not salvation. For this task we will need not just shame and guilt, but empathy: the capacity to vividly imagine the experiences of others, both present others, perhaps in distant places, and non-existent others, including our own future selves. We must be spurred to new levels of individual and community resilience and to new modes of cooperation on climate action. Adaptation to global climate catastrophe will not be easy.

In this chapter, I focus on the prophetic power of storytelling, considering American audiences in particular. I mention many kinds of stories: family lore, tales of old and new ecological heroes, science fiction novels, naturalist poetry, and more. I explore two fictional prophetic stories in some depth: the American Dust Bowl narratives of John Steinbeck's *Grapes of Wrath* and Sanora Babb's *Whose Names Are Unknown*, both of which have resonance in light of our contemporary circumstances. I focus specifically on their fictions of expanding social consciousness in times of shared vulnerability. Admittedly, the prophetic rhetoric of these stories might not move everyone. As I said, we need many prophets: diverse storytelling for diverse audiences is necessary in the fragmented moral and epistemic space of modernity.

Family Storytelling and Resilience

In a series of studies, Emory psychologist Marshall Duke and his colleagues have looked at how family storytelling practices and awareness of family stories contribute to the well-being and resilience of children and families. On a scale that Duke and his colleagues refer to as the "Do You Know (DYK) Scale," children and adolescents with strong family narrative scores showed "higher levels of self-esteem, an internal locus of control (a belief in one's own capacity to control what happens to him or her), better family functioning, lower levels of anxiety, fewer behavioral problems, and better chances for good outcomes if a child faces educational or emotional/behavioral difficulties."[5] The resilience impacts of family storytelling are

4. McGrath, "Twelve Years to Save the Planet?"
5. Duke, "Stories That Bind Us," para. 1.

not limited to personal trials. One group of Duke's research participants was scored both before and after 9/11. Participants who knew more about their families better managed the stress of community-wide trauma too.[6]

Family stories, Duke and his colleagues believe, generate resilience not from knowledge of the answers to "Do You Know" questions, but from long-term practices of reinforcing healthy emotional attitudes and frameworks through storytelling.[7] The sharing of family narratives shapes an "intergenerational self," an awareness of one's historical relationship to prior generations who struggled with their own challenges.

Duke's research is suggestive: stories of the right kind, told in the right ways, exercise empathetic imagination in the service of self and other-awareness and resilience. Though family stories are not strictly speaking prophetic, they often function as moral examples, recounting failures, heroism, and humor or cleverness in the face of adversity. My own grandmother's penny-pinching during the Depression and as a single mother during World War II was, for my family, an account of her character, her debt savvy, and why she continued well into her eighties to squirrel away sugar packets from restaurant tables. She adapted, and so can we. Thus, family stories may function as near-prophetic parables of readiness for whatever may come our way.

As we stand on the edge of twenty-first-century environmental catastrophe—runaway global warming, mass extinction of animal and plant species, acidifying oceans, flooding, wildfires, agricultural losses—there is no better time to build intergenerational selves and resilience. Still, while family story-telling practices may be a good place to start, why stop there? Might other kinds of stories have similar resilience-building powers?

Prophetic Storytelling in a Larger World

As Jonathan Lear recounts in his book *Radical Hope*, while Crow leader Plenty Coups was still a boy, he had a dream-vision in which the buffalo were swallowed up by the earth and traditional Crow lands were despoiled. Plenty Coups's dream was ominous, a sign of unthinkable change to come, but Crow leadership noted in it a reason for hope: the Chickadee, a Crow wisdom symbol, also appeared in Plenty Coups's vision:

---

6. Feiler, "Stories," paras. 20–21.
7. Duke, "Stories That Bind Us," para. 4.

> He [the Chickadee] is least in strength but strongest of mind ... He is willing to work for wisdom. The Chickadee person is a good listener. Nothing escapes his ears ...Whenever others are talking together of their successes and failures, there you will find the Chickadee-person listening to their words.[8]

Lear credits the Chickadee symbol with helping to sustain Crow life in a time of unprecedented change. If the Crow were to survive the encroachment of white European settlers, intensifying conflicts with neighboring tribes, and eventually forced relocation to reservation lands, they needed to listen like the Chickadee, make wise decisions, and adapt to new circumstances.

And this the Crow did, though life for them changed dramatically. They pragmatically sided with the United States Army in the Indian Wars. They maintained access to some of their traditional tribal lands, though shrunk by orders of magnitude under the thumb of the American government. Plenty Coups himself became a farmer rather than a roaming warrior-hunter.[9] In their Chickadee-wisdom, the Crow survived, though the very core of Crow life—visions of the good life, practical and moral virtue—were turned upside down in the process.[10]

Or consider the story of Noah, similar in many respects despite a distance of culture and religion. With transcendental guidance for the construction of an Ark—a symbol of salvation—Noah and kin survive God's cataclysmic flood. In larger community with the nonhuman species they have preserved, they enter into a new covenantal relationship with God to replace the old, damaged one.[11] After the flood, God tells Noah of the Rainbow, a symbol of hope and a reminder to both God and humanity of their new covenant.[12]

Noah's village, his friends, and his home are gone. Washed away are the landscapes he knew as a boy and the trails he took to the market. According to one rabbinical text, the flood required God to keep Noah childless late into his life, otherwise he would have needed supplies to build

---

8. Lear, *Radical Hope*, 80.

9. "Chief Plenty Coups."

10. I want to be careful not to introduce false equivalencies. Unlike most Americans in our contemporary climate emergency, the Crow were not suffering, or imposing on others, the costs of their own, or their forefathers,' environmental sins; their threats were largely external.

11. Gen 5–10.

12. Gen 9:13–17.

many arks.[13] Rebuilding has complications too. Noah will plant a vineyard, get drunk, and his son Ham will sin against him, cursing some of Noah's descendants to remain in perpetual slavery.[14] As with the Crow, we can ask: What resilience must Noah and his family have had? They adapt, but the Ark and Rainbow are not without costs.

Traditionally, prophecy, which Amy Merrill Willis has usefully described as "fore-telling, truth-telling, and forth-telling," involves a prophet anticipating the future incipient in an existing, compromised moral order.[15] Prophecy is often reserved for shamans and seers and specially-appointed prophets whom God or the gods have touched with otherworldly insight. In late modernity, prophetic voices are approached with skepticism, perhaps as suspicious modes of self-divination rather than divine election. As a result, we have an unprecedented need for higher truth and for the authoritative voice to speak it and, simultaneously, an unprecedented level of disagreement about the sources of truth that are authoritative. If only, perhaps, our God or gods could speak to us in our ways, convey to us the harms we have done to the planet, and demand of us a change, albeit one that will remain compromised and difficult.

Of course, they have, in a sense, through an entire repository of human stories and story-telling arts that profoundly and prophetically expands our limited vision. George Shulman, in *American Prophecy: Race and Redemption in American Political Culture*, appeals to story-telling, in particular, as a mode of reenchanting us to the prophetic imagination:

> Visionary storytelling by those who bear witness seems ever more essential: To name the constitutive exclusions, amnesia, and anxious dream of sovereignty that make imperial power and repressive action seem credible answers to wounded national identity. The office of those who bear witness is not only critical or disenchanting, though, for by passionate language that seizes audiences, prophetic testimony can make dead bones live. Prophecy can elevate people's "expectations and requirements," Thoreau says, by animating values they imagine as static, dramatizing commitments they reify by forgetting, and energizing democratic solidarities they invoke in name only. In these and other ways, prophetic visions, questions, claims, demands, and

13. Gen. Rab. 26:2.

14. Ham's sin depends on the meaning of "seeing his father's nakedness" in Gen 9:22. See Goldenberg, "Ham," 257–65.

15. Willis, "Once There Were Two Men"; Willis, "How to Be a Prophet."

energy—provoking, recalcitrant, haunting, passionate, and poetic—may be especially needful now.[16]

Prophetic visions may come to us through stories—family stories, religious stories, even fictional stories—to move us, to 'make dead bones live' à la Shulman. As Merrell Willis points out, stories also have a way of disarming us: they cue our capacities for empathy and fellow-feeling even before we identify ourselves with the characters or narratives at play in them.[17] On one hand, it is a challenge that we live in the most symbol-rich time in all of human history. The multiplicity of symbols creates noise; it is all too easy to ignore important things and binge on fluffy entertainment. On the other hand, the diversity and reach of storytelling has never been greater, and the power of storytelling arts to evoke emotion, imagination, and empathy remain strong.

So, in addition to our family sagas, we have Plenty Coups, and Noah and other biblical prophets. Might there be value in the telling and retelling of their stories? Or might, instead, a twenty-first-century Plenty Coups/Noah emerge with a twenty-first-century Chickadee/Ark/Rainbow? Sixteen-year-old climate activist Greta Thunberg was recently reported to be sailing to New York to attend climate talks because flying is too carbon-intensive.[18] Margaret Atwood's *Oryx and Crake* or Emily St. John Mandel's *Station Eleven* offer harrowing science fiction stories of adaptation to catastrophic environmental change. Add in naturalist essays and poetry, from Thoreau's *Walden* to Gary Snyder's *Turtle Island*. Are these our many prophets? Can they prime our imaginations, invite us to experience the world through others lenses, enlarge the self, intergenerationally and interculturally?

---

16. Shulman, *American Prophecy*, xvi.

17. Willis, "Once There Were Two Men."

18. Friedman, "Greta Thunberg to Attend." From Greta Thunberg's Ted Talk "School Strike for Climate": "If I live to be 100, I will be alive in the year 2103. When you think about the future today, you don't think beyond the year 2050. By then, I will, in the best case, not even have lived half of my life. What happens next? The year 2078, I will celebrate my 75th birthday. If I have children or grandchildren, maybe they will spend that day with me. Maybe they will ask me about you, the people who were around, back in 2018. Maybe they will ask why you didn't do anything while there still was time to act. What we do or don't do right now will affect my entire life and the lives of my children and grandchildren. What we do or don't do right now, me and my generation can't undo in the future." Thunberg, "School Strike for Climate," 6:54—8:00.

Wanting Prophecy

Dust Bowl Stories and Climate Refugees

Polling suggests that Americans are increasingly open to climate urgency, though only 51 percent are what Gallup describes as "concerned believers."[19] When we look closely at ourselves, and our neighbors, and, beyond, to the rest of the world, it is notably business as usual. Philosopher Caspar Hare refers to our situation as a climate-based "Prisoner's Dilemma," in which "some of us are individually better off, short term, driving SUVs, but if we all emit carbon like crazy, we're all worse off than if none of us do."[20] The only way to break out of the dilemma is through trust and cooperation: we would all be safer if we jointly, significantly reduced our carbon emissions, yet no one wants to make changes to their own lifestyle if others are not doing the same.

Many partial solutions to global warming have been proposed, from carbon taxes to carbon sequestration, from government regulation to reengineering the atmosphere. Echoing the language of the prisoner's dilemma, cultural critic Roy Scranton calls it a "wicked problem": "Global warming ... doesn't offer any clear solutions, only better and worse responses. One of the most difficult aspects to deal with is that it is a collective-action problem of the highest order. One city, one country, even one continent cannot solve it alone."[21] While scientists and policy makers continue to appeal to scholarly and scientific consensus, critics like Scranton cry, "We're fucked."[22]

Global temperature increases locked in by carbon emissions since the beginning of the Industrial Age guarantee us that our lives will change in the coming decades. While rapidly greening our carbon-based economies would be traumatic too—as if we could take fossil fuels out of our lives and keep everything else intact!—failure to implement aggressive, globally-cooperative climate action will create a new and chaotic world order. Much of the world faces current immigration challenges, some of them already climate-based. What happens when every vulnerable person living in a coastal/waterfront and tropical/semi-tropical area around the globe must leave home? Where will they go? How will they get there? And in what manner will they be treated when they arrive?

---

19. Saad, "Americans as Concerned as Ever," para. 10.
20. Zimmerman, "Prisoner's Dilemma," para. 4.
21. Scranton, *Learning to Die*, 53.
22. Scranton, *Learning to Die*.

Perhaps family stories and tradition-based symbols like the Chickadee or the Ark could work here, but other prophetic voices might speak more fully to the plight of environmental refugees. I have in mind, specifically, tales from the American Dust Bowl of the 1930s. Dust Bowl stories are largely about white, Midwestern, American farmworkers, which may be important for a contemporary American cultural imaginary in which migrants have only brown or black skin, and refugees are foreigners. Could Dust Bowl stories help us to see ourselves fictionally as migrants, if not to imagine ourselves as *actual* migrants-in-the-making?

The most famous of fictionalized Dust Bowl stories comes to us from John Steinbeck, in his masterly novel *The Grapes of Wrath*, published in 1939. A lesser-known novel, Sanora Babb's *Whose Names Are Unknown*, had its contract for publication rescinded in the same year, when publishers decided that Steinbeck had satisfied public desire to read about Dust Bowl migrants. Babb's novel was not published until 2004. Like *The Grapes of Wrath*, Babb's story is laced with prophetic symbols, language in the mood of moral judgment, and calls to social action. Though fictional, both stories are worth telling and retelling for their power to resituate the self in a broader intergenerational and intercultural context.

According to historian James N. Gregory, 300,000 to 400,000 people from Plains states such as Oklahoma, Arkansas, Missouri, and Texas moved to California in the 1930s.[23] Half of these Plains migrants were from rural areas, and naturally looked for work in agricultural zones like California's San Joaquin Valley. Theirs was the story made iconic by Steinbeck's Joad family, though it was told by others too, including Babb, who was a California journalist at the time.[24]

The overarching narratives of Steinbeck's and Babb's novels are likely familiar: an Oklahoma family and some friends, evicted from their own farmsteads during the leanest years of the Dust Bowl, pile all their remaining possessions into an old jalopy and travel west for California. They have never seen California before; all they know is what they have heard, which is that it is a land of plenty, a new Eden, and that there is dignified farm work to be had there. They start to hear murmurs on the road, in makeshift roadside camps of fellow travelers: California is overrun with outsiders;

23. Gregory, "Dust Bowl Migration," para. 5.
24. Gregory, "Dust Bowl Migration," para. 7. Gregory also points out (para. 6) that 95 percent of the Plains migrants were white, which made them a promising object of national sympathy, unlike the laborers of Mexican and Asian descent who had long been toiling in California fields.

Californians do not want them; there is even a name for their type, "Okie." ("Okie," one of Steinbeck's traveling strangers tells the Joads, "use' ta mean you was from Oklahoma. Now it means you're a dirty son-of-a-bitch. Okie means you're scum. Don't mean nothing itself, it's the way they say it.")[25] Having nothing to return to at home, they press on, only to discover that conditions are worse than they had imagined. The plots of Steinbeck's and Babb's novels diverge, especially once their protagonists reach California, but they share something important despite it. They tell of displaced people, whose treatment is a source of expanding social consciousness, both for the characters themselves and for their readers.

At the opening of Steinbeck's novel, Tom Joad, one of the grown Joad boys, returns home from prison to find his family home abandoned. Tom's folks, along with his grandparents, his five siblings, and his sister's husband Connie, are at his Uncle John's house, packing up for their westward trek. Tom meets former preacher Jim Casy on the way to find them and invites Casy along.[26] In brief vignettes interspersed between longer plot-driven chapters, Steinbeck offers sketches of archetypal bank managers, police officers, tractor drivers, and used car salesmen who have turned on their fellow Oklahomans. In a characteristic passage, Steinbeck's imagined car salesman unleashes all his excuses:

> Sure, we sold it. Guarantee? We guaranteed it to be an automobile. We didn't guarantee to wet-nurse it. Now listen here, you—you bought a car, an' now you're squawkin'. I don't give a damn if you don't make payments. We ain't got your paper. We turn that over to the finance company. They'll get after you, not us. We don't hold no paper. Yeah? Well you jus' get tough an' I'll call a cop. No, we did not switch the tires ... He bought a car, an' now he ain't satisfied. How'd you think of I bought a steak an' et half an' try to bring it back? We're runnin' a business, not a charity ward.[27]

---

25. Steinbeck, *Grapes of Wrath*, 205–6.

26. Casy has been thinking about human solidarity for a while. Foreshadowing the social awareness that emerges in the novel, he tells Tom, "I figgered, 'Why do we got to hang it on God or Jesus? Maybe,' I figgered, 'maybe it's all men an' all women we love; maybe that's the Holy Spirit—the human sperit—the whole shebang. Maybe all men got one big soul ever'body's a part of.' Now I sat there thinkin' it, an' all of a suddent—I knew it. I knew it so deep down that it was true, and I still know it." Steinbeck, *Grapes of Wrath*, 24.

27. Steinbeck, *Grapes of Wrath*, 65.

Babb tells a similar story of community unraveling, but in tragic or elegiac tone, rather than Steinbeck's darkly humorous and cynical voice. Milt and Julia Dunne and their children, along with some neighbors, abandon their farm for new opportunities out west. Babb details the environmental, physical, and social conditions of the years leading up to their departure. She writes with sympathy for the Dunnes and for farm life, especially its sense of ritual and expectation:

> In September the winter wheat was planted. Milt and the old man rose every morning at daybreak. Julia was up before them, building the fire and getting the coffee and oatmeal ready. While they were eating the oatmeal, she fried them each two eggs and gave them thick pieces of the bread she baked one day in the week. There was butter, but not to be used generously or it would not last until the next churning. In the dugout it was still dark, and the men ate by lamplight. When they came up into the yard, the sharp high air of western autumn came into their noses, penetrated their clothes, made them go about their chores briskly. Each morning they felt renewed in themselves and a clear unknown excitement sprang up in them with the sense of the new season . . . The men spoke of the wheat, of the weather they needed. A freeze. Snow through the winter, to lie on the fields, to sink into the ground below the roots so the young plants could withstand the dry summer days. A little spring rain. No hail. No hot winds. No year would be as certain and perfect as this, but every season the dryland farmers hoped for one thing, feared another, and breathed again in relief if the crop was still safe.[28]

At the beginning of Babb's novel, three generations of Dunnes are living in a one-room dugout house. Food grows scarcer with each passing season. The Dunnes slide from modest frugality to miserable want. Milt is ready to steal a neighbor's starving animal to feed his family. Lacking nutrition, Julia loses a baby. A local merchant kills himself rather than calling in farm debts. Eventually, the dust defeats them:

> The dirt had dropped . . . like a curtain. He [Milt] looked at his wheat and his face tightened. The smell of dust was strong in their noses now, slapping their senses like a thick fat hand. 'Look!' he said again, and they stood together not saying anything, awed by this new attack of nature. It was an evil monster coming on in mysterious, footless silence . . . Grains of dust sounded against their

---

28. Babb, *Whose Names*, 6.

shoes in a low flurry. The open land was blotted out as the brown mass struck the edge of his field.[29]

Steinbeck's Joads and Babb's Dunnes leave everything behind for a chance at a better future. They do not see this future as a zero-sum game, but one in which there will be plenty for everyone to share. They take neighbors and acquaintances with them; they gain new friends as they travel. On the road, those friends become "family":

> In the evening a strange thing happened: the twenty families became one family, the children were the children of all. The loss of home became one loss, and the golden time in the West was one dream. And it might be that a sick child threw despair into the hearts of twenty families, of a hundred people; that a birth there in a tent kept a hundred people with the birth-joy in the morning. A family which the night before had been lost and fearful might search its goods to find a present for a new baby.[30]

By the time they arrive in California, the travelers have lost family and gained them. They are penniless and starving. The largest farms are shrinking wages and gouging workers for goods at their farm stores. Henchmen harass migrant workers to keep them from getting comfortable while making sure they stay long enough to get the harvest in.

Babb's protagonists' sense the expansion of their social selves. Milt Dunne comes to regard himself and other migrant farmworkers as deeply, fundamentally the same. Milt sees Mexican migrant workers "work[ing] for nothing for the same reason we do."[31] He recognizes that he is no different from a black worker he meets in the field: "We're both picking cotton for the same hand-to-mouth wages. I'm no better'n he is; he's no worse."[32] Babb voices the Dunnes's new social consciousness in clearly prophetic language:

> South to north the valleys curved in a long green flowering bowl, filled with food enough for a nation, while hunger gnawed these workers' bodies and drained their minds. An old belief fell away like a withered leaf. Their dreams thudded down like the over-ripe pears they had walked on, too long waiting on the stem. One thing was left, as clear and perfect as a drop of rain—the desperate need

---

29. Babb, *Whose Names*, 78.
30. Steinbeck, *Grapes of Wrath*, 193.
31. Babb, *Whose Names*, 180.
32. Babb, *Whose Names*, 185.

to stand together as one man. They would rise and fall and, in their falling, rise again.[33]

Tom Joad senses it too. He and preacher Casy become involved in farm labor organizing, at great cost to themselves and their families. Tom tells his Ma: "I been thinkin' a hell of a lot, thinkin' about our people livin' like pigs, an' the good rich lan' layin' fallow, or maybe one fella with a million acres, while a hunderd thousan' good farmers is starvin'. An' I been wonderin' if all our folks got together an' yelled …"[34]

Fictionalized Dust Bowl narratives such as Steinbeck's and Babb's give their readers an imaginative glimpse of life upended. Hardworking, poor, mostly white farmers sacrifice everything familiar to them to migrate for work. In terms of what Duke and his colleagues call the intergenerational self, readers of Dust Bowl stories can understand themselves in historical relation to the characters' suffering: What did my parents, grandparents, or great grandparents do during the Depression? What happened in my town or community during the 1930s? How did people work together, and how were they divided? Perhaps individual and family resilience in the face of rapid global warming can be cultivated in this way, as fictionalized narratives remind us of nonfiction truths about our own immigrant, farming, or even Dust Bowl family histories.

The possibilities for enlarging readers' intercultural selves are obvious too. Treatment of the "Okies" takes on new meaning in light of the Trump Administration's southern border control policies, separating families and detaining people in inhumane camps. If literature can help us imaginatively identify with the plight of Dust Bowl migrants like the Joads and the Dunnes, perhaps it can help us feel for the migrant family from Honduras or El Salvador, to see the courage and resilience of people who have acted in circumstances that are not of their choosing, with consequences that will most likely mean an end to their familiar ways of life. Could our own sense of family, or our hospitality for the migrant traveler, be stretched by the act of reading (or listening or watching)? More powerfully still, might some of us even begin to see ourselves in the story, not as heroes, but as their foes: directors, officials, policy makers, and business owners who have strayed from our moral ideals?

---

33. Babb, *Whose Names*, 222.
34. Steinbeck, *Grapes of Wrath*, 419.

Wanting Prophecy

Public Prophetic Arts

Human activities, from the way we manufacture and purchase goods, to how we eat, travel, and heat and cool our homes—really, what choices can we make without climate consequences?—have caused the Earth's atmosphere to warm at an alarming rate, melting polar ice caps, acidifying oceans, changing weather patterns, and contributing to the loss of millions of animal and plant species. The window for a global, cooperative response to global warming is rapidly closing.

To raise up diverse, climate-sensitive, prophetic voices is not necessarily to call people back to church, temple, or mosque, though religious communities continue to be at the forefront of American rituals of storytelling, and at least some of those communities are ready to be environmental leaders. I have suggested that narrative, storytelling, and the arts more broadly have an essential role to play in late modern prophecy, working on their audiences from the inside out, spawning empathy and imaginative identification with fictional and actual others. I have suggested that we may be helped toward cooperation and resilience by these stories. We might find ourselves or our families in them, recognize our complicity or our inaction, or begin to imagine a future in which we too are environmental refugees, one of Babb's "unknown names."

Regardless of venue (church, temple, mosque, elementary school, college, art museum, public square, etc.), I suggest we put new and old media to use in an intentional practice of sharing stories with wide and diverse resonance for Americans whose lives must soon change. A new folk storytelling festival movement would be a great start, but we need prophetic narratives from our families, our ethnic and religious traditions, and our writers and poets, to be told more frequently and celebrated more fully at home, on television, and in other public or community forums too. Public prophetic art and arts may prepare us not just in the sense of coping with unchosen loss or change, but in encouraging us to overcome hopelessness and dismissal, to contribute to a future that is, by intention, different from our past: more just in its distribution of goods and opportunities; more hospitable in its treatment of others; and more cooperative in its protection of the land, its animal inhabitants, and its human populations, especially the most vulnerable among us.[35]

---

35. Sommer, *Art in the World*.

The illustrations I have offered—whether hearing our grandparents tell of family sacrifice, sharing a resilience parable from a cultural or religious tradition, or encountering a Dust Bowl story—have no exclusive prophetic power. Regional or community-centric narratives, of, say, return to New Orleans in the aftermath of Hurricane Katrina or organizing a response to flooding along canals and flood plains in Miami, might prove to be potent reminders of the need for intergenerational and intercultural selfhood within particular cultural spaces and for particular audiences. For the late modern prophetic imagination, no single symbol will suffice. To be sure, some audience members will be too caught up in self or distracted by others to really listen. However, while empathy can be "banal," as Namwalli Serpell recently argued in *The New York Review Books*, it can also be transformative: "Art should not be a release valve, but a combustion engine."[36] It is time to rev those engines.

No one can predict what an intentional practice of enhancing our environmental prophetic imaginary will do to or for us: what kind of life it will call us to pursue in all of its particulars, how much comfort we will need to give up or how often we will need to protest. Yet, the failure of empathy to enlarge the self, to instigate cooperation and resilience, will be much, much worse. We need prophets, in our own families and in public forums as well, and we need to be ready to respond to their arts, as they call us to act with resilient courage, imagination, and hope to voluntarily risk the end of a comfortable, familiar, protected way of life . . . before that life is chaotically brought to an end for us.

---

36. Serpell, "Banality of Empathy," para. 36. Serpell argues that empathy can be self-serving and that we too readily praise the empathy powers of narrative arts. At the same time, Serpell distinguishes between cognitive and emotional forms of empathy, defending the cognitive type: "This [cognitive empathetic] way of relating to others is not just tourism. Nor is it total occupation—there is no 'assimilation' of self and other. Rather, you make an active, imaginative effort to travel outside of your circumstances and to stay a while, where you're welcome" (para. 25).

5

Post-Katrina Prophecies

Lisa Woolley

The destruction caused by Hurricane Katrina could be understood as prophetic—in the everyday sense of predicting the future—in that it represents the deadly convergence of climate change, degradation of natural protections against high winds and flooding, neglect of infrastructure, and the failure of private industry and every level of government to adequately prepare for or respond to extreme weather. Instead this essay addresses the role of prophecy in literary efforts to remember this hurricane's devastation, for we cannot improve in the future without remembering the past and honoring all that was lost. In her reflections upon recovering from Katrina, Natasha Trethewey reminds readers that "rebuilding is also about remembering—that is, not just rebuilding the physical structures and economy of the coast but also rebuilding, revising, the memory of Katrina and its aftermath."[1] Art and literature serve this process of remembering Hurricane Katrina, grieving the resulting losses, and learning from them.[2]

---

1. Trethewey, *Beyond Katrina*, 20.
2. A year after Hurricanes Katrina and Rita in a special issue of *Callaloo* that included interviews, photographs, poems, short stories and essays, Carl Lindahl categorized mostly by length and genre the first efforts to represent the devastation. In their introduction to *Ten Years after Katrina: Critical Perspectives of the Storm's Effect on American Culture and Identity*, Mary Ruth Marotte and Glen Jellenik also discuss the literary genres that have emerged to represent Katrina, and they identify three waves of literary development: "Katrina as Event," "Katrina as Fallout," and "Katrina as Springboard" (x).

Prophecy too in the American tradition can be understood as learning from the past in order to rebuild during a time of crisis. In *American Prophecy: Race and Redemption in American Political Culture,* political theorist George Shulman examines how prophetic discourse has become secularized in western culture in general and in American culture in particular.[3] Two novels that remember Katrina, *Hold It 'Til It Hurts* (2012) by T. Geronimo Johnson and *Salvage the Bones* (2011) by Jesmyn Ward, engage in a secularized form of the prophetic known as lamentation, which involves finding meaning in suffering.

Like many authors before them, Johnson and Ward adapt the prophetic discourse that has been woven into US history to a current emergency. Shulman explains that prophets who lament "ask and answer the question, What is the meaning of our suffering? They help people endure catastrophe and exile by *poetry* that endows a painful history with meaning. From Jeremiah's lamentations to the sorrow songs and spirituals of slaves and their heirs, the office of prophecy is to voice traumatic loss and hopes of redemption."[4] Shulman discusses the "extraordinary elasticity" of the prophetic in terms of "translation" from one context to another,[5] but in the case of the two African-American novels under discussion here, improvisation might serve as a more fitting metaphor for the authors' adaptations of lamentation. Examining the importance of jazz to Toni Morrison's *Beloved,* Shulman concludes that she "commemorates a traumatic history and the vernacular forms that transfigure it."[6] Rather than emulating the form of jazz, as Morrison's novels often do, Johnson and Ward make improvisation critical to their novels' plots and their characters' efforts to understand the significance of surviving Katrina. The two novels contrast, however, when the characters tell stories lamenting their losses. *Hold It 'Til It Hurts* warns against a rush to find redemption, whereas *Salvage the Bones* illustrates

---

3. Shulman examines three forms of the prophetic genre: theodicy, jeremiad, and lamentation. He reexamines the role of the prophetic in American politics and expresses reservations due to its deployment to dominate and exclude vulnerable groups of people (*American Prophecy,* ix–x). At the same time, however, the writers he examines (Frederick Douglass, Henry David Thoreau, Martin Luther King, James Baldwin, and Toni Morrison) also have used the prophetic mode to challenge white supremacy (*American Prophecy,* xii).

4. Shulman, *American Prophecy,* 5–6.

5. Shulman, *American Prophecy,* 232.

6. Shulman, *American Prophecy,* 191.

lamentation through characters who confront trauma in the process of finding collective meaning in catastrophe.

While the American authors Shulman explores lament a history of "traumatic dispossession,"[7] Johnson and Ward focus primarily on the immediate displacement Hurricane Katrina causes, although the losses fit a pattern of uprooting African Americans and other ethnic minorities in the United States.[8] The characters improvise first for the sake of physical or psychological survival and then for the sake of remembering traumatic events. Rebecca Solnit finds the former kind of improvisation critical in her analysis of responses to calamities in *A Paradise Built in Hell: The Extraordinary Communities that Arise in Disaster*. She assesses the legacy of Katrina and sees murdering vigilantes, fear-mongering media, and injudicious officials[9] but also large numbers of people responding "with generous improvisations to save themselves and others."[10]

By "improvisations," Solnit means taking action in the absence of an official plan or using materials in unconventional ways. In African American fiction, the term takes on a special resonance, particularly in the context of lamentation, where prophets give meaning to a painful history. Discussing improvisational music in her foreword to *Jazz*, Morrison writes, "Whatever the truth or consequences of individual entanglements with the racial landscape, the music insisted that the past might haunt us, but it would not entrap us."[11] Morrison's formulation captures the binaries that structure both improvisation and lamentation: haunt/entrap and individual/us. Her instructive linking of past and present, moreover, connects jazz and other African-American forms of music to lamentation and imagines improvisation as both a practical skill and an assertion that the past's collective survival guides change in the present. Ralph Ellison explains jazz musicians' attention to both past and present as

> the desire to express an affirmative way of life through its musical tradition and . . . this tradition insisted that each artist achieve his

---

7. Shulman, *American Prophecy*, 11.

8. See, for example, Clark and Lloyd. Dyson discusses Hurricane Katrina through the lens of race, poverty, and theodicy. For a discussion of Katrina within an environmental justice framework, see, for example, Johnson and Rainey and Bullard. Two and a half years after Katrina, Bullard cited the death toll as "1,836, and still counting" ("Differential Vulnerabilities," 753).

9. Solnit, *Paradise Built in Hell*, 235–66.

10. Solnit, *Paradise Built in Hell*, 267.

11. Morrison, *Jazz*, xvi.

creativity within its frame. He must learn the best of the past, and add to it his personal vision. Life could be harsh, loud and wrong if it wished, but they lived it fully, and when they expressed their attitude toward the world it was with a fluid style that reduced the chaos of living to form.[12]

Although their focus on sorrow or celebration varies, Ellison, Morrison, Solnit, and Shulman all emphasize individuals or small groups who turn a history of suffering into life-sustaining assistance or meaning for the benefit of a larger community. In *Hold It 'Til It Hurts* and *Salvage the Bones*, mourning becomes lamentation, that is, a genre of the prophetic, when authors and characters improvise to create narratives. These novels challenge forms of consolation that do not fully measure the damage or enable others to make sense of their own suffering, to give form to the chaos of living.

Born in New Orleans, Johnson narrates his first novel, *Hold It 'Til It Hurts*, in third person from the main character, Achilles', point of view. Achilles's return from two tours of duty in Afghanistan serves as the personal and national context of Hurricane Katrina. Achilles and his brother, Troy, arrive at their rural home north of Hagerstown, Maryland, and learn that, while they were en route from Afghanistan, their father died in a car accident. Mr. Conroy's funeral replaces their welcome home party, and then their mother honors her estranged husband's wishes by presenting her adopted, African American sons with envelopes containing information about their birth parents. Achilles refuses to open his because he considers his white parents his only parents, but the next morning, Troy and his envelope have vanished.

Eventually, Achilles hears from a member of his army unit who has seen Troy in New Orleans. There Achilles learns that the men from his unit are struggling to reintegrate into civilian life, an experience he compares to "hitting the ground without a chute."[13] To look for Troy, Achilles volunteers at social service agencies and meets Ines, a community activist and former volunteer with an NGO operating in Afghanistan. The mirror opposite of Achilles, who has dark skin but little connection to black culture, Ines appears white but comes from a family with deep roots in New Orleans. Throughout his odyssey, Achilles deceives his mother, his friends, and Ines by failing to correct mistaken impressions, as when Ines assumes

---

12. Ellison, "Living with Music," 189–90.
13. Johnson, *Hold It 'Til It Hurts*, 302.

they share the same inimical relationship to white Americans. Because he has withheld different information from different people, his life becomes fragmented due to the necessity of preventing friends from meeting each other. Achilles cannot lament the losses he has endured because he refuses to construct a narrative about himself, the war, or his place in American civilian life in which others can share.

Throughout much of the novel, Achilles's denial of mutual suffering prevents him from finding meaning in the surrounding chaos, yet Johnson is not blaming the victim. Johnson has described his main character as "not yet able to process" all that he has been through—Katrina, the war, his childhood in a multiethnic family.[14] Achilles's failure to articulate the truth as he knows it, however, undermines his reason for coming to New Orleans. Nearly a year later, Achilles hears from another member of his Army unit, who has spotted Troy in Atlanta. There Achilles finds Troy's belongings in the possession of some homeless drug addicts and then finds his body in a morgue, although he cannot bring himself to identify him officially. When Achilles at last returns to the morgue, Troy's ashes are filed only by date of cremation, which Achilles does not know. Meanwhile, Hurricane Katrina has struck New Orleans, and Achilles returns to find Ines's ancestral home serving as a combination phone bank, soup kitchen, and homeless shelter. Achilles embeds himself with a National Guard unit and at first saves the stranded but, like many of the rescuers, is quickly reassigned to apprehending suspected looters and tossing bottled water to those waiting on bridges and rooftops. This unofficial rejoining of the military creates the allusion of familiarity, which further confuses Achilles's attempts to make sense of his own actions and of the country to which he has returned. Shulman writes that "prophets make claims about the circumstances and difficulties—and fateful decisions—*of the whole*; indeed, in this way they reconstitute the very 'we' they seem to invoke as a given."[15] Achilles, in contrast, struggles with a sense of isolation, finding no whole to which he can belong—others' stories do not seem to include him, and despite his experiments with assembling the pieces of his experience into a coherent narrative, he cannot formulate a story that includes them. Put in terms of Ellison's description of jazz, Achilles has not yet developed his personal vision or connected it to a tradition.

---

14. Dalamangas, "Interview," para. 4.
15. Shulman, *American Prophecy*, 6.

Achilles has not turned his grief to lamentation because he cannot yet give his story a form within the context of the nation's trauma in Afghanistan and New Orleans. Shulman asks about prophecy, "Is the political task to enable a 'mourning' by which the dead can bury their dead, or to avow and live within, not leave behind, constitutive losses?"[16] Johnson addresses the same question in narrating Achilles's response to Troy's death, which he hesitates to acknowledge and then to explain truthfully. As Achilles's suffering increases in the year following his discharge from the military, he switches from passive to active deception. This trend peaks when Achilles is searching the New Orleans morgues for Ines's grandfather, finds a severed hand with a scar similar to the one in Troy's palm, and claims the hand, which is sent to Maryland for a military funeral.[17] Achilles is now eager to bury his brother, rather than learn to live with the loss by raising questions within a community about Troy's death, the victims of Katrina, and the deaths of other veterans. Shulman argues that "critics of white supremacy use prophecy to forge a politics that mediates part and whole to reconstitute community."[18] Achilles plays the opposite role by deceiving several communities. He disingenuously allows the hand to become a synecdoche, a literary device in which a part substitutes for the whole, that is, to stand for the suffering of New Orleans and the Gulf Coast. Burying the hand in Maryland represents a naïve gesture to resolve national dysfunction by forgetting it.

Achilles fabricates a story linking an unidentified, dismembered victim of Katrina and Troy's heroic military service in hopes of redeeming Troy's life, and by extension the war and the inept official response to Hurricane Katrina. The preacher at Troy's funeral easily embellishes Achilles's fictitious lamentation and, for Achilles and readers at least, offers false consolation:

> . . . Troy, *We all know, was a believer, for rarely did a man make better use of his talents. Rarely did a man make so selfless a sacrifice with heart and head.* With a grand gesture, the minister pointed

---

16. Shulman, *American Prophecy*, 36.

17. For further analysis of the symbolism of violence to black bodies and counternarratives to it, see Clark's examination of *Salvage the Bones* in a Southern context of abandoning victims of racial violence, Lloyd's exploration of "the throwaway bodies of the South" (246) in *Salvage the Bones* and *Beasts of the Southern Wild*, Crownshaw's discussion of these bodies in relation to testimony, and Rankine's analysis of the display of slain black bodies in the civil rights movement and the killings sparking Black Lives Matter.

18. Shulman, *American Prophecy*, 25.

to the military photo mounted on an easel next to the coffin, describing Troy as a veteran who selflessly served abroad and at home, who fought to bring freedom to Afghanistan and safety to Louisiana, who exemplified Christian ideals *in life and in death*.[19]

While Achilles failed to share his initial processing of the war with others, this public tale of redemption too easily unifies through a story others are eager to accept. Johnson is not mocking the mourners at Troy's funeral; they are responding with love to a story they have no reason to disbelieve. As stand-ins for the American public, however, we readers must be wary of hearing what we want to hear in explanations of misfortune.

In this case, lamentation is not synonymous with comfort, for the accurate version of Troy's death would bring little relief to his friends and family, and stories like it should haunt a nation remembering Katrina and still at war. Shulman writes that prophets "declare truths we avoid at great cost to ourselves and others. Prophecy is the office that announces the reality of what (and who) we had not counted as real, that 'remembers' what we forget or refuse to see."[20] Achilles's solution to his reluctance to identify Troy—substituting the hand instead of admitting that his remains cannot be claimed—does not allow mourners to ask the difficult questions about why Troy became an illegal drug user in the pursuit of a deeper sense of his own identity. As proxies for his fellow American citizens, though, readers are urged to see, among other issues, returning veterans, racial disparities, and the need for equitable disaster planning. In one form or another, too many vulnerable Americans are "hitting the ground without a chute,"[21] a state of affairs that, if unchanged, will diminish us all.

Although untrue, Achilles's lamentation nevertheless serves several redemptive purposes in the novel. Generosity of sorts motivates Achilles's improvisation upon what has actually happened. First, because of her accumulated losses, Mrs. Conroy cannot endure the news that Troy has died due to his involvement with ruthless drug dealers, and Achilles mercifully invents a story that makes her loss bearable. Second, the unknown man who died following Katrina is claimed as a brother, in every sense of the word. Third, although he died as a homeless drug addict, Troy earned a bronze star and deserves the honor of a military funeral. Achilles himself served honorably in Afghanistan and then volunteered in New Orleans, so

---

19. Johnson, *Hold It 'Til It Hurts*, 328–29.
20. Shulman, *American Prophecy*, 30.
21. Johnson, *Hold It 'Til It Hurts*, 302.

the story he invents for Troy has some basis in reality. Fourth, upon returning to Maryland and participating in Troy's funeral, Achilles understands for the first time the solidarity among the veterans in his hometown. Finally, because Ines accompanies Achilles to Troy's funeral, he at last tells her the truth about his family, Troy, and the past year, and Johnson holds out the possibility that Achilles may begin the journey toward self-acceptance upon which he has refused to embark since reluctantly volunteering for the US Army.

Lamentation, however, has not been historically a matter of individual consolation. In joining a dismembered hand that represents Louisiana to Troy's murder, which exemplifies the alarming death rate for returning veterans, Achilles avoids traumatic facts and *misremembers* Hurricane Katrina and the war in Afghanistan. In other words, Achilles's story improperly reconstructs the fragmented body politic, stitching together hopeful accounts of the war on terrorism and the response to Katrina. By Shulman's standard of "media[ting] part and whole to reconstitute community,"[22] Achilles is not yet serving as a prophet; he is preserving existing bonds but not deepening a shared understanding based on a reckoning with the war and the hurricane. Writing about Black Lives Matter, Claudia Rankine's reflections on mourning seem applicable to *Hold It 'Til It Hurts* when she writes that the movement "aligns with the dead, continues the mourning, and refuses the forgetting in front of all of us."[23] Despite some good emerging from Achilles's deception, at this point in the novel, he contributes to personal and national forgetting.

Rather than looking away, Johnson's own lamentation, in the form of the novel itself, offers a clear-eyed account of twenty-first-century suffering. Throughout the novel, Johnson presents examples of both true and failed lamentation. Comparing the combat zone to the home front becomes a crucial step in making meaning. Achilles thinks to himself, for example, "no blue cords, no silver wings—prepared them for the actual devastation on the ground in Afghanistan: the odd children's sandal amidst the rubble, the leveled towns, rank subterranean jails, marble-eyed refugees, the constant odor of death.... [Afghanistan], however, adequately prepared Achilles for the Gulf Coast."[24] *Hold It 'Til It Hurts* prompts readers to reflect upon the role of the military in both locations as the war in Afghanistan lengthens.

22. Shulman, *American Prophecy*, 25.
23. Rankine, "Condition of Black Life," 151.
24. Johnson, *Hold It 'Til It Hurts*, 265–66.

As we have seen, even though Achilles is accepted while on active duty in the military, re-enacting that role in New Orleans does not prompt him to grieve in a way that makes his and the nation's losses meaningful. Moreover, he is stopped daily as a suspected looter, and civil authorities in New Orleans prevent ordinary civilians from saving others.[25] Johnson writes, "[L]aw enforcement waved his military ID through roadblocks where civilian volunteers towing boats and campers were turned away."[26] This official response represents the opposite of improvisation, creating powerlessness for the sake of an agenda that does not address the misery.

Johnson presents brief moments of improvised democracy in relation to Ines's family's efforts to serve their community. Solnit writes that small-scale volunteer efforts are often more nimble than large, centrally-organized relief efforts.[27] "Citizens themselves in these moments constitute the government—the acting decision-making body—as democracy has always promised and rarely delivered," she writes.[28] After Katrina, Achilles reacts to Ines's house, which used to intimidate him:

> Inside was another world, but a different world from what he remembered. Taking in refugees had given the house life and purpose. Gone were the aprons, housekeeping dresses, and smocks. Gone were the tuxedoes and propeller ties and chef toques. Gone was the livery dressed as if to grieve. The staff wore casual clothes, which ironically only heightened the sense that the house was in mourning.[29]

This picture of grief in action contrasts with Ines's accusation that Achilles's "grieving voice sounds exactly like your lying voice."[30] Lamentation, in contrast to false consolation, is not an easy form of personal solace; neither does it fabricate a narrative that masks the reality

---

25. In her autobiographical account of surviving Katrina in Mississippi, Ward reports encountering no officially organized relief for days, and then finding water from "a private driver, not attached to any federal or state campaign." From him she learns about resources mainly directed to guarding large retail stores ("We Do Not Swim in Our Cemeteries," 38). As Solnit asks, "[W]ho cares if electronics are moving around without benefit of purchase when children's corpses are floating in filthy water and stranded grandmothers are dying of heat and dehydration?" (*Paradise Built in Hell*, 238).
26. Johnson, *Hold It 'Til It Hurts*, 266.
27. Solnit, *Paradise Built in Hell*, 299.
28. Solnit, *Paradise Built in Hell*, 305.
29. Johnson, *Hold It 'Til It Hurts*, 303.
30. Johnson, *Hold It 'Til It Hurts*, 272.

of suffering at home and abroad or denies the inadequacies of American democracy. Instead, Johnson represents a house that has changed, and those who work in it have renewed authority and commitment.

Finally, by juxtaposing Afghanistan and New Orleans, Johnson compels readers to ask why American society has become such a difficult place to which to return. In *The Iliad*, the city of Troy survives the Greeks' siege but is defeated by the gift of a wooden horse. In *Hold It 'Til It Hurts*, the character Troy survives combat but not his journey to re-establish himself at home. Resisting market pressure for writers of color to formulate agreeable endings, Johnson attests, "I write for the ones who didn't get away . . . if our society does not face these narratives, we will keep writing them—in bone, on flesh."[31] Johnson brings to mind what Cornel West has referred to as "an aggressive pessimism" that casts doubt upon "the possibilities of fundamental transformation" in American society but in a way that "becomes sobering rather than disenabling."[32]

Johnson's lamentation nevertheless offers a glimpse of how redemption might look. Early in the novel when Achilles begins looking for Troy, he meets Father Levreau at a soup kitchen and finds the priest and his church rather pathetic. "Of all the prophets Levreau had mentioned," Achilles thinks, "out of the entire Old Testament starting lineup, Achilles recalled only Jacob and Noah. Jacob he didn't know, but everyone knew Noah . . ." Back on the streets of New Orleans, Achilles thinks, "If ever a city needed a Noah."[33] In contrast, after the flood, Achilles finds the fragments of New Orleans precious. A chance encounter with a mail carrier Achilles used to find irritating, for instance, leads to a lengthy conversation about their families and current situations in New Orleans.[34] Perhaps Achilles's memory has shifted unconsciously from Noah to Jacob—not the flawed figure's sibling rivalries but his declaration in Genesis 28:16, "Surely the Lord is in this place; and I did not know it."[35] Referring to the traits of "altruism, mutual aid, and the ability to improvise," Solnit writes that "disasters do not generate them; they are constructed by beliefs, commitments, and

---

31. Dalamangas, "Interview," para. 14.
32. West, "Prophetic Tradition in Afro-America," 41–42.
33. Johnson, *Hold It 'Til It Hurts*, 84.
34. Johnson, *Hold It 'Til It Hurts*, 310.
35. Revised Standard Version. Thanks to Father David Gunderson for his reflections on this passage over the years.

communities, not by weather, seismology, or bombs."[36] After Katrina, hope for redemption, Johnson laments, lies not in a triumphant narrative but in a renewed sense of belonging to our desolated environments, whether they are ruined cities or eroding small towns.

In contrast to *Hold it 'Til It Hurts*, *Salvage the Bones,* Mississippi-born Jesmyn Ward's second novel, is narrated by a first-person female narrator and set in only one county in Mississippi over just twelve days. Pregnant fifteen-year-old Esch and the rest of the Batiste family are preparing to ride out Hurricane Katrina on their rural property known as the Pit, which includes both their home and their abandoned maternal grandparents' house. Ward represents the Batistes as doing the best they can to prepare for Hurricane Katrina, given their relative isolation and poverty, but their pre-hurricane routine has deteriorated in recent years because large storms have veered away and because Esch's mother has died following childbirth. The novel's secularized lamentation of Katrina begins with Esch's efforts to understand what is happening to her, expands to reunify her family, and then finds meaning for increasingly larger communities.

In a sense, the Batistes' preparations represent a false confrontation with the power of hurricanes—a failure of the prophetic—in that the family has not recognized the extraordinary degree to which they will need to look out for one another. Esch's father, Claude, has become chemically dependent; her oldest brother, Randall, is focused on earning a scholarship to basketball camp; her older brother Jason, known as Skeetah, is obsessed with dog fighting; and his beloved pit bull, China, has just given birth to six puppies. Their preoccupations leave Esch with most of the responsibility for her youngest brother, Junior, who crawls under the house in a search, as Mary Ruth Marotte suggests, for "some womb-like dwelling in which to heal."[37] Marotte notes that Claude has drilled his children about what to do in the event of a hurricane but "remains as withdrawn from them as he has been since Mama's death."[38] When not consumed with longing for her unborn child's father, generically named Manny, Esch is reading Edith Hamilton's *Mythology* in preparation for eleventh grade. Esch is especially enthralled by Medea, who falls madly for Jason and then kills their children and his betrothed after he spurns her. As the hurricane nears, Randall is thrown out of the decisive basketball game when Skeetah and his friends

---

36. Solnit, *Paradise Built in Hell*, 302.
37. Marotte, "Pregnancies," 209.
38. Marotte, "Pregnancies," 210.

create a disturbance, their father tears off three fingers while repurposing the chicken coop, some of the puppies die, Esch battles morning sickness, Manny cruelly rejects her when she reveals her pregnancy, and when sent to the store with money to buy non-perishable food, Skeetah purchases two fifty-pound bags of dog food, and seemingly as an afterthought, some canned peas and ramen noodles. The family nevertheless proceeds with responsible preparations.

Ward stresses the Batistes process of finding meaning in and after Hurricane Katrina; in fact, most of the novel is narrated in present tense. Although initially the family's improvising mainly takes the form of a practical skill, Ward's lamentation also emphasizes the role of learning from tradition as the characters remember, tell, and revise family stories that warn and reassure them about hurricanes. Acting with what Solnit would call "generous improvisations to save themselves and others,"[39] the Batistes think quickly when a nearby creek floods their home during Katrina. They break through the roof and climb an oak tree to the grandparents' abandoned house that sits on just enough of a rise that its attic is dry. In this endeavor, Claude discovers that Esch is pregnant and accidently pushes her into the rushing water. As Skeetah jumps in to help Esch, China falls out of the sling he has made from his pants. Thanks to their ability to improvise, the humans survive, although China swims out of sight. For the family, redemption from the storm will involve sacrifice and forgiveness.

Ward puts the Batiste family's improvised escape from the water in the context of an African American history of survival. In jazz, improvisation means more than invention; it means creating something new within the outlines of another composition. Like the artist, who must "learn the best of the past, and add to it his personal vision,"[40] the characters use the grandparents' house whenever they must fix or replace something in their own house. Taking things from the original dwelling at the Pit not only saves money but also represents the forebears' continued guidance, literally through supplying materials and figuratively through the example of their resilience, so it is fitting that the Batistes survive by fighting their way to this structure. This ancestral home thus symbolizes their family's legacy of surviving slavery, Reconstruction, the civil rights era, and turn-of-the-millennium capitalism and therefore provides shelter from the storm.

---

39. Solnit, *Paradise Built in Hell*, 267.
40. Ellison, "Living with Music," 189.

Unlike Achilles in *Hold It 'Til It Hurts*, then, Ward's characters are not simply inventing stories in lamenting Katrina; they are generously *improvising* to save themselves and others. Although Rose Batiste is dead, her stories continue to instruct her children and guide their response to the hurricane. Esch remembers that, while comforting the children during Hurricane Elaine, Rose passes on her memories of the legendary Hurricane Camille. After describing the destruction, odor, and death toll, Rose recalled that

> she and Mother Lizbeth walked miles for water from an artesian well. She said she got sick, and most everybody did, because even then the water wasn't clean, and she had dreamed that she could never get away from water because she couldn't stop shitting it or pissing it or throwing it up. She said there would never be another like Camille, and if there was, she didn't want to see it.[41]

Although Rose tells this story to reassure her children, she does not omit the painful details. In her dream, contaminated water has blurred the boundary between the inside and the outside of the human body. Clearly Rose's story will have to be updated after Katrina, but it remains relevant in its prophetic warning about a hurricane's power and, in keeping with the discourse of lamentation, has turned the family's suffering into life-sustaining assistance for the benefit of future generations.

Unlike *Hold It 'Til It Hurts*, which accentuates a dismembered body, *Salvage the Bones* features a dissolving body that threatens to merge with its watery environment. Several scholars have commented upon Ward's blurring of boundaries in the novel.[42] Crownshaw, for example, discusses its "systematic indistinction and slippage between human, animal, and environment."[43] Images of unstable categories and threatened dissolution abound as both humans and animals prepare for the hurricane, the hurricane is personified, and the flooded stream is compared to a snake. The destruction of a nearby town is described as the bay's having "swallowed the back of St. Catherine, and vomited it out in pieces,"[44] making the wreckage of the built environment indistinguishable from bodily fluids.

---

41. Ward, *Salvage the Bones*, 218.

42. See also Clark and Lloyd for discussions of blurred boundaries in the novel. In "Pregnancies, Storms, and Legacies of Loss in Jesmyn Ward's *Salvage the Bones*," Marotte analyzes comparisons between Esch and the pitbull China.

43. See Crownshaw, "Natural History of Testimony," 170.

44. Ward, *Salvage the Bones*, 252.

Esch describes her family after the storm abates: "We were a pile of wet, cold branches, human debris in the middle of all the rest of it."[45] Here Esch, unlike Achilles, fully confronts the extent of her losses before attempting to redeem the situation. Shulman writes that prophetic discourse involves a "vision of internal and worldly transformation,"[46] but it does not "disavow the darkness surrounding us."[47] According to her description, Esch's family has indeed been transformed, changed into another category of existence; metaphorically they are temporarily reduced to damaged plant life, nearly indistinguishable from the other kinds of wreckage that surrounds them.

The hope of redemptive transformation in Ward's lamentation comes from a renewed sense of community in the towns of Bois Sauvage and St. Catherine. Much as the dismembered body in *Hold It 'Til It Hurts* reflects the divided American public, the dissolving body in *Salvage the Bones* represents the momentary lack of difference between black, white, Asian, rich, and poor citizens, who all struggle to comprehend their losses. Solnit writes, "The joy in disaster comes, when it comes, from that purposefulness, the immersion in service and survival, and from an affection that is not private and personal but civic: the love of strangers for each other, of a citizen for his or her city, of belonging to a greater whole, of doing the work that matters."[48] In keeping with this spirit, the Batiste family is taken in by Randall's friend Big Henry and his family, where adults tend to Claude's wound. Esch dissuades her brothers from beating up Manny, the young people share their Ramen Noodles with an elderly stranger, and they explore the coastline and return with stories of the damage. Re-engaging his family, Claude discusses the need for prenatal care with Esch. Big Henry assures Esch that her child will have many protective fathers in the community, and families sit down to a communal meal. As Ward writes in her earlier, autobiographical account of Katrina, after walking around the neighborhood checking on one another, "We were barefoot and muddy and tired, but, we confirmed, alive, alive, alive, alive."[49]

Unlike in *Hold It 'Til It Hurts*, where Achilles's initial mourning of Troy's death often contradicts Johnson's lamentation, Ward's main character appears to speak for her, even though the outlines of her story are

---

45. Ward, *Salvage the Bones*, 237.
46. Shulman, *American Prophecy*, 232.
47. Shulman, *American Prophecy*, 253.
48. Solnit, *Paradise Built in Hell*, 306.
49. Ward, "We Do Not Swim," 36.

different than Ward's own. While surveying the damage in St. Catherine, Esch engages in a two-part lamentation that will enlarge the Batiste family's body of hurricane lore. Her first motivation is to include Skeetah, who has stayed behind at the Pit to await China's possible return, in the community's wider story. She collects broken glass and stone from the debris and imagines telling Skeetah, "*This was a liquor bottle,* I will say. *And this, this was a window. This, a building.*"[50] Esch's lamentation grows beyond her individual processing of the hurricane to encompass the rest of her family.

Additionally, Esch wants to pass on her experience with Katrina to the next generation, so she envisions turning the fragments into a mobile: "I will tie the glass and stone with string, hang the shards above my bed, so that they will flash in the dark and tell the story of Katrina."[51] This project seems like a singularly bad idea in a displaced household preparing for a baby, but the image of a mobile recalls the community's acts of improvisation. It preserves the memory of brokenness but transforms it into art. In keeping with Ellison's description of improvisation, Esch is lamenting Katrina "with a fluid style that reduce[s] the chaos of living to form."[52] Mobiles move, and the relationship between the parts is reconfigured, just as the meanings of the stories change slightly with each new hurricane and the relationships between members of the community are reconceived. As with *Hold It 'Til It Hurts,* the audience must engage in the process of seeing the connections between the fragments of the characters' lives and their relationship to the readers' own world.

In the second part of the lamentation, Esch states her understanding of the hurricane, improvising upon several stories in western culture.[53] She sees Katrina as Medea,

> the mother that swept into the Gulf and slaughtered. Her chariot was a storm so great and black the Greeks would say it was harnessed to dragons. She was the murderous mother who cut us to the bone but left us alive, left us naked and bewildered as wrinkled newborn babies, as blind puppies, as sun-starved newly hatched baby snakes. She left us a dark Gulf and salt-burned land. She left us to learn to crawl. She left us to salvage. Katrina

---

50. Ward, *Salvage the Bones,* 254.
51. Ward, *Salvage the Bones,* 255.
52. Ellison, "Living with Music," 190.
53. For discussions of Greek and Roman mythology in the novel, see Locke, "Of Fury and Furies," and Crownshaw, "Natural History of Testimony," 172.

is the mother we will remember until the next mother with large, merciless hands, committed to blood, comes.[54]

Esch's lamentation revises the figure of either a wholly nurturing or irrationally destructive Mother Nature and replaces her with a birthing parent. Furthermore, Esch has decided to name the baby, if a boy, after her brother Jason, replacing the story of Medea's family tragedy with one of survival. Finally, Esch's words faintly echo those of another pregnant girl who prophesies, who proclaims that God "has put down the mighty from their thrones, and exalted those of low degree; he has filled the hungry with good things, and the rich he has sent empty away."[55] Both Mary and Esch are awed by an almighty power; Esch's lamentation, however, does not include anyone's being exalted, only everyone's being reduced to crawling and scavenging. The "we" in her lamentation of Katrina at first refers to the Batiste family but expands to include the whole Gulf coast and perhaps the entire Earth. Shulman writes, "Fundamentally, prophets rework political identification to create a collective subject for whose fate members are liable and from whose fate none are exempt."[56] According to Esch's prophecy, violent storms will reduce *all of us* to salvaging the bones.

Prophetic or not, novels alone do not transform the world. As Joseph Donica reminds us, "No organization bases its post-disaster policy on the recommendation of those in literary studies."[57] Shulman himself is wary of prophecy and its role in a democracy but he asserts that prophetic language "remains the only legitimate public language for addressing the character and fate of the whole. No one owns it; it is available for reworking in politics."[58] Solnit echoes Shulman in claiming that "the language for prizing eros and domesticity has never been stronger, and the language for public life more atrophied."[59] Moreover, this essay synthesizes pre-2016 work by Shulman, Solnit, Johnson, and Ward, perhaps casting further doubt on the efficacy of the prophetic mode in furthering positive change. The record of protecting the vulnerable before and after violent storms post-Katrina, for example, has been mixed. Novels, however, do have the potential to change readers, especially if authors' revisions of disaster narratives shape their

54. Ward, *Salvage the Bones*, 255.
55. Luke 1:52–53 (RSV).
56. Shulman, *American Prophecy*, 33.
57. Donica, "Disaster's Ethics," 11.
58. Shulman, *American Prophecy*, 233.
59. Solnit, *Paradise Built in Hell*, 306.

audience's practical, moral, and emotional responses to the next tumultuous event. As Donica writes, "Literature rarely has real-world consequences, but this is what gives literature its power. The reader is the intended subject upon which literature acts."[60] Rather than forgetting the results of racism and poverty, readers of the literature remembering Katrina continue to be haunted by unfathomable losses. Spending hundreds of pages with Achilles and Esch entangles us in these characters' anguish, but it does not entrap us in past conflicts. Instead Johnson and Ward urge us to move forward by honestly addressing our own pain while attending to the needs of our neighbors. By engaging in lamentation, *Hold It 'Til It Hurts* and *Salvage the Bones* enlarge the language of public life by creating a shared interest in the nation's dismembered and dissolving bodies. While recognizing that the consequences of wars and catastrophes are not shared equally, both novels address the meaning of collective suffering, suggesting readers' and writers' mutual responsibility for remembering, rereading, and reworking our stories of survival and our shared fate.

60. Donica, "Disaster's Ethics," 11.

6

The Prophet Samuel R. Delany

Vincent W. Lloyd

Hope animated the US civil rights movement of the 1950s and 1960s. Black Americans felt moved by a dim possibility of equality, and that movement brought together millions to march and organize for an end to racial discrimination. The movement's anthem, "We Shall Overcome," and its most famous oration, "I Have a Dream," put hope front and center. Catalyzing this movement and stoking feelings of hope were prophetic figures: Black ministers preaching that injustice ran against God's will, that hope for justice was divinely authorized.

There are many differences between the racial justice movement that grew around the hashtag Black Lives Matter and the civil rights movement, but among these the absence of talk about hope is particularly striking. Love and commitment, even faith, are present in movement discourse, but, if anything, hope has been replaced by disappointment as a starting point for organizing. That disappointment is sometimes filled out with the theoretical idiom of Afropessimism, holding that anti-Black racism is constitutive of the metaphysics of the West, that assimilating Blacks to the figure of the slave is essential to the functioning of the modern world. If anything is to be hoped for, from this perspective, it is "the end of the world."[1]

---

1. Frank Wilderson, who coins "Afropessimism," develops this account of "the end of the world" from views put forward by Aimé Césaire and Frantz Fanon. Wilderson, *Red, White, and Black*, 74, 337.

Believing that there is no hope for Blacks in the world, no hope for assimilation or substantive equality, means the language and practice of today's racial justice movement looks quite different than the movement of a half century earlier. Christianity does not provide an idiom, values, or institutional base for the movement. And the movement is not catalyzed by preachers of hope; the emphasis is on developing a "leaderful" rather than "leaderless" movement, utilizing the capacity of all rather than a select few to lead. Indeed, those associated with Black Lives Matter often criticize the civil rights movement for placing excessive focus and responsibility on Black male preachers, noting the gender and sexuality dynamics at work in privileging such figures, as well as the implied commitment to "respectability politics" that compromises Black demands in the interest of appeasing white anxieties (with those anxieties sometimes internalized by the Black community).[2]

Is there a role for prophecy in this new racial justice movement? Before addressing this question directly, it should be noted that the language of "futures," particularly "Black futures," does play an important role in the discursive world of Black Lives Matter—and in some important ways supersedes the language of hope. In addition to the use of the phrase "Black futures" on social media, it has taken institutional form. Three women coined the phrase "Black Lives Matter" in 2013, and two years later the network of grassroots groups that they founded began promoting February as Black Futures Month. Along with remembering outstanding Blacks of the past, February was also to become a time for Black communities to collectively imagine what the world could be like. Black Futures Month "imagine[s] a future in which Black people are fully liberated. A future where our opportunities are abundant, we are thriving, and our lives are safe from police violence . . . where we are seen and valued as our full selves."[3] One of the Black Lives Matter cofounders, Alicia Garza, started a spin-off non-profit, the Black Futures Lab, dedicated to helping Black communities imagine together and then plan what policy changes could be made to bring that future closer to reality. Inhabiting a novel kind of prophetic office, Black activist and cultural worker Adrienne Maree Brown and her sister, Autumn Brown, host a podcast titled *How to Survive the End of the World* that features a

---

2. For a scholarly account of these concerns, see Edwards, *Charisma and the Fictions of Black Leadership*.

3. For information on the 2020 Black Futures Month, see https://blacklivesmatter.com/how-do-you-envision-a-black-future/.

broad array of movement leaders and attracts a wide audience interested in imagining justice-filled futures. Both Brown sisters are involved in science fiction writing in addition to their curating and activism. Adrienne Maree Brown writes, "Science fiction is simply a way to practice the future together. I suspect that is what many of you are up to, practicing futures together, practicing justice together, living into new stories. It is our right and responsibility to create a new world."[4] While Autumn Brown describes herself as a "theologian," Christianity is rarely mentioned on their podcast, though a broader sense of spirituality pervades it.[5]

A prophet, from the perspective of racial justice movements today, may look more like a science fiction writer than a polemicist or Christian preacher. To try out this hypothesis, and to examine what it may mean for our understanding of prophecy, this chapter turns to Samuel R. Delany. While Delany is best known for his widely acclaimed science fiction writing, he is also a critic, memoirist, musician, queer theorist, filmmaker, and, as a documentary film about him proclaims in its title, "polymath."[6] Delany is also a Black American, and he writes on race, though not exclusively on race. This chapter focuses on a discrete set of his work, his three memoirs, particularly his third, querying what it might mean to consider this text prophetic, and what that might mean for justice movements in the present. This analysis shows that Delany offers a paradigm of democratic prophecy suited to our current cultural and political moment. First, though, we will examine what might be called the standard account of democratic prophecy, so we can see how this account might need to be reconsidered in light of Delany's example.

The Quest for Democratic Prophecy

Over the last few decades, social critics and political theorists have developed resources for thinking about prophecy in a democratic context. This does not necessarily mean a secular context; rather, it means a context that rejects authoritarianism. In such views, the prophet cannot simply channel the word of God to the masses, nor can the prophet generate on her own extraordinary insights (paradigmatically, about the future) to which

---

4. Brown, *Emergent Strategy*. See also the collection of activist reflections inspired by Black science fiction writer Octavia Butler: Brown and Imarisha, *Octavia's Brood*.

5. Autumn Brown studied theology at Oxford and General Theological Seminary.

6. Taylor, *Polymath*.

others then conform their lives. These would be forms of authoritarian prophecy, with the few (or the one) imposing their views on others. Sacvan Bercovitch, Michael Walzer, George Shulman, and others have sought to retain the essential features of the figure of the prophet, from Biblical, religious, and broader cultural contexts, while describing the prophet as at home in a democratic culture.[7]

The democratic prophet is situated in a community, among the people. She is not at the center of the community, nor is she outside a community; she is at a community's edges, formed by and attached to that community but also noticing its inconsistencies. Specifically, the democratic prophet notices the way that a community's current practices mismatch that community's core values. The prophet publicly decries this mismatch, perhaps in a speech, perhaps in a novel, perhaps in a painting. Prophets excel when they effectively discern core values, perceptively notice mismatches, and persuasively share their conclusions. But none of this work is as straightforward as it at first seems. The wealthy and powerful conceal the ways that current community practice actually advances their interests instead of a community's core values. The prophet, then, must attend to such dynamics, particularly evident in contexts of marginalization. When the prophet speaks about the needs of a marginalized community, she is not affirming that a community values the marginalized; the prophet is showing that, as a prerequisite to determining a community's core values, systemic anti-democratic distortions of that community must be rectified. The rhetorical mode that prophets in the Jewish and Christian traditions, and in cultures influenced by those traditions, tend to employ is the jeremiad, condemning a society for its shortcomings (with respect to core values) and promising rewards in the future (the land of milk and honey) if corrections are made.

Clearly this model of democratic prophecy fits with standard accounts of the US civil rights movement. Someone like Martin Luther King called those in the US to change their present practice (segregation) in line with a core value of the nation (equality), and his speeches and writings also highlighted the ways in which attention to a particularly marginalized segment of the (American) community, Black Americans, could shed light on systematic distortions of that community's values. But in the current era of racial justice organizing, this model of democratic prophecy falls short.

---

7. Bercovitch, *American Jeremiad*; Walzer, *Interpretation and Social Criticism*; Shulman, *American Prophecy*.

What the (American) community genuinely values, all the way back, is white supremacy, or so the claim goes. If this is the case, attention to Black experience by a prophetic critic would not so much reveal the machinations of a privileged few but would, rather, simply demonstrate that a majority of the community is, indeed, committed to preserving its privileges. Finally, from the perspective of Black Lives Matter–associated organizing, it remains an open question whether the democratic account of prophecy could ever be sufficiently democratized. The role of one who threatens punishments and promises rewards, even if the basis of these claims is a community's own values, may itself be inextricable from authoritarianism—in the confidence it gives to some (including the prophet) about moral uprightness and in the vulnerability it casts on others (even those with privilege in some respects may be marginal in other respects).

Is it possible to shift from the model of a prophet who offers hope for those who will convert to righteousness and condemns the wicked to a prophet who catalyzes the collective imagining of futures without oppression? Such a prophet would have to avoid the moralizing that goes along with dividing the damned and saved and would have to avoid the optimistic belief that every community's core values, discerned through its history, stand opposed to domination. The opposition to domination in the new form of prophecy could not come by fiat (unmediated revelation), lest the new account of prophecy devolve into another form of authoritarian prophecy. And the new form of prophecy would have to encourage multiple, varied visions of a future without domination, not a singular vision of one particular land of milk and honey.[8] To see whether this might be possible, we turn to Samuel R. Delany.

Heavenly Breakfast

Delany was born in 1942, in New York City. His grandfather was born in slavery and eventually became a college administrator and Episcopal bishop. His father was a funeral director, and his family was part of the emerging Black middle class. Delany was a brilliant student, attending the renowned Bronx High School of Science (where he was a classmate of Stokely Carmichael) and beginning to write novels as a teenager. In 1961 he married his Jewish high school classmate Marilyn Hacker (who would go

---

8. As David True helpfully pointed out, Shulman's account of democratic prophecy pushes in this direction.

on to become a renowned poet). Hacker was pregnant, and Michigan was the nearest state that permitted interracial marriages of people their age, so they took a bus to Michigan for their nuptials. While Delany and Hacker remained married until 1980, from the 1960s the center of Delany's life became queer spaces and relationships. His first novel would be published in 1962, and he would publish one or two books a year over the coming years.[9]

Delany wrote science fiction, but his fiction also crossed genres, and it consistently explores issues of gender, race, and class. For example, the story "Aye, and Gomorrah," published in 1967 and winner of that year's Nebula Award for best science fiction story, imagined a world where humans needed to be neutered in order to go into deep space in a narrative that takes place in France, Turkey, and the United States. In this story and others, Delany probes what it means to be aware of our desires, and aware of the inability to have all of our desires fulfilled.[10] He reports that his literary influences range from nineteenth-century British literature to James Baldwin. In addition to his literary output, Delany also writes, lectures, and teaches as a literary critic, and in that capacity he engages broadly with contemporary philosophy and theory, including such thinkers as Quine, Wittgenstein, Derrida, and Foucault.

Delany's prolific writing offers ample opportunities for exploring what it might mean to read his work as in some sense prophetic, but also offers an intimidating number of possible starting places. This chapter focuses on Delany's autobiographical writing because those texts combine reflection on his utopian longings with critical inquiry into unjust social structures which he confronts. Also, he explicitly or implicitly responds to shifting cultural and theoretical currents as he re-writes his life in his three memoirs, published in 1978, 1988, and 1999. Throughout, Delany wrestles with questions of community and its exclusions, and in each case Delany writes for a broad audience, calling his readers to interrogate their own lives and the forms of community in which they participate.

The first of Delany's three memoirs, *Heavenly Breakfast: An Essay on the Winter of Love*, offers sketches from the life of a commune in which Delany lived during winter of 1967–68. While the book is written in the first person and draws on Delany's journal from the time, he describes it as a composite and condensation of multiple times, people, and experiences. The literary

---

9. For biographical information, see, for example, Freedman, "Samuel Delany," 398–407.

10. Delany, *Aye, and Gomorrah*.

crafting of the text is guided by its purpose: the book's introduction makes clear that this "essay" is intended to interrogate the idea and practice of communal living. And, as the book's subtitle hints, it is meant to complicate how we understand 1967's Summer of Love in our collective imagination. That year was supposedly filled with youths partaking in newfound sexual freedom while listening to rock and roll, lazing around parks and communes. As the book opens, Delany complicates this image with more events: the assassination of Martin Luther King, the assassination of Robert Kennedy, and the attempted murder of Andy Warhol. *Heavenly Breakfast* aims not simply to be an exposé of the commune, showing its darker side, as it were, but to interrogate the very ideas that animated the project of communal living.

What Delany finds most endearing about the commune ideal that Heavenly Breakfast (name of both commune and the band who were its primary inhabitants) exemplifies is that it calls into question how we understand community and the requirements for communal living. "The Heavenly Breakfast was not particularly democratic," he opines (15). There were no meetings, no votes, no mission statement, no visioning sessions. There was not even a sense that decisions were to be driven by consensus, or that membership came with responsibilities and benefits. But, a dozen, or perhaps two dozen, young people (the average age was twenty-two) lived together in an apartment in a way that did not result in significant harm to any of them, and probably benefited many of them. There was minimal privacy—a bath in the kitchen, no door to the bathroom, a bedroom shared by all—but it was, according to Delany, not hard to be alone. He reflects that when one lives with a large group, it is always possible, with simple body language, to indicate that one is not available for conversation, whereas in a group of two or three there is a constant obligation to participate in conversation. There were health problems, including an outbreak of gonorrhea, but there were also people around watching out for each other's health.

Most basically, Delany describes how the commune's norms developed organically, in response to individuals' problem-solving and innovations. Someone noticed the floor was getting dirty. They cleaned it and asked people to take their shoes off. A norm was established of taking one's shoes off upon entry to the Heavenly Breakfast. More generally, "If you wanted something done, you did it; if you wanted people to do something, you asked them. The goad to do something someone wanted you to do was having to live with that person's discomfort or disapproval if you didn't do it. As close as we lived, that was quite a goad" (15). Witnessing the particular desires and needs of others motivated and constrained each individual's actions. Visitors who did not appreciate this would not be welcomed to stay at the Heavenly Breakfast. Its governing principle about interpersonal relations, and intimate relations especially, was: "Not to take offense at someone else's desire. If it pleases you, you move toward it; if not, you sidestep politely as your individual temperament allows" (20). The complexity and fluidity of individual desires was never subsumed into a whole; the commune was simply the site at which those desires were negotiated. Delany observes, "There was nothing terribly collective about it" (15). While residents would choose any of the six beds they liked to sleep in, and there was a good deal of interpersonal intimacy, each person had a bundle of clothes that was their own, and people had their own typewriters, musical instruments, and other equipment—though they could be borrowed, when desires aligned.

And it was all fueled by a desire for human flourishing. Such flourishing is not be captured by the "value metrics" that talk of sex and drugs tends to attract. Instead, Delany's book aimed to capture "the texture and affectivity of life lived humanely, day to day." Delany insists that this is a political sensibility, even as it is not captured by the usual political categories of capitalism or socialism, war or peace. And it is fueled by desire: "This book is dedicated to who ever did anything no matter how sane or crazy, whether it worked or not, to give themselves a better life." Flourishing requires experimentation, and these experiments will often be fleeting.[11] Each of these experiments is educational, producing qualitatively better knowledge for living than any amount of acculturation in one's own home community. Delany provides plenty of contrastive examples about poor experimentation. One commune is so counter-cultural it has no electricity, no cooking, and constant quarrels; another is so bourgeois each person has their own room, some with televisions, and dinner is served nightly on a grand dining table. The Heavenly Breakfast is just the right size and shape to permit an experiment in life lived humanely.

The Motion of Light in Water

Delany's account of the Heavenly Breakfast can sound utopian, like a sophisticated sort of utopianism that incorporates the tragic and

11. Compare Wolin, "Fugitive Democracy."

acknowledges its own precariousness. Tavia Nyong'o suggests that we should attend to Delany's prose: its controlled minimalism resists attempts to read it as straightforwardly and exhaustively referential; its focus on "ambient poetics" and "musicking" encouraging us to focus on the performance of an ensemble rather than the demands of an identity group.[12] This stands in sharp contrast to Delany's next memoir, *The Motion of Light in Water: Sex and Science Fiction Writing in the East Village*, which features Delany's characteristically thoughtful prose but is also prolix to the point of promising exhaustiveness and accuracy. In this second memoir, the site of utopian potential shifts from an apartment to New York's gay bathhouses and other sites where gay men gather for sex.

Delany details, with a surveyor's eye, the features of the bathhouses and his own experiences at them. But now, rather than exploring a fleeting utopian ideal, the ostensible purpose of Delany dwelling on the bathhouses is to detail how they contributed to a sense of gay identity that individuals could then inhabit. In the bathhouses he encountered "an undulating mass of naked, male bodies, spread wall to wall," bodies that collectively proved "there was a population—not of individual homosexuals . . . not of hundreds, not of thousands, but rather of millions of gay men, and that history had, actively and already, created for us whole galleries of institutions, good and bad, to accommodate our sex" (293). Delany and others previously had inclinations toward homosexuality, intuitions that constantly struggled against, and troubled, homophobic social norms. But in encountering the bathhouses, these men could unequivocally embrace their gay identity, and power. "Whether male, female, working or middle class, the first direct sense of political power comes from the apprehension of massed bodies" (293). Experiencing the bathhouses was uncontestable evidence, not only of the existence of gay people but that there must be more, there must have always been more, and they must have always been finding each other, even in repressive conditions. To give language to this experience, Delany argues, is to potentially transform the possible forms of life: it can make tolerable what was once marginal and vulnerable.

The feminist historian Joan Scott, clearly taken by Delany's precise and lucid prose and powerful political argument, chooses *The Motion of Light in Water* as an exemplary instance of minority narrative gone wrong. The error lies in the narrative strategy, she contends, that leans on "the evidence of experience": "What could be truer, after all, than a subject's own account

12. Nyong'o, "Back to the Garden," 758.

of what he or she has lived through?"[13] Writing in 1991 at the height of the multiculturalism boom, and public contest over multiculturalism, Scott worries (from the political left) that the emerging fields of identity studies purport to build themselves on the bedrock of individual experience, but this bedrock is less solid than it, at first, seems. By naming, in the first person, his own gay experiences and those of people around him, Delany seems to be establishing the foundation for affirming gay identity (and history, and public culture). Scott's worry is that such a narrative strategy focuses on the individual at the expense of the social. Why and how did a society exclude gay people in the first place? Further, if we bracket the identity label ascribed to participants in bathhouse culture, might we not find individuals negotiating complex desires and social structures in more subtle ways than the label "gay" would allow? Finally, Scott queries, doesn't the focus on personal experience "reify agency as an inherent attribute of individuals," rather than seeing resistance flowing collectively, caught in a dance with social forces?[14]

Even if one accepts Scott's point about narrative strategies, it is not clear that *The Motion of Light in Water* is quite as susceptible to this line of critique as Scott makes it seem. While Delany's expansive prose does seem to promise referentiality in a way that his sketches in *Heavenly Breakfast* do not, in both works the narrative advances through sketches broken into short sections. Indeed, the passage Scott points to is a theoretical reflection interspersed between narrative sketches in Delany's book, not a description of his first-person experience itself. Moreover, the fragmentary accounts of experience are not linked together by one overarching theoretical framework; rather, Delany appeals to equally fragmentary theoretical resources to illuminate them—for example, in one place reflecting on what Freud would illuminate, in another place reflecting on what Marx would illuminate. In short, Delany's second memoir is structured quite differently than the sorts of narratives grounded in individual experience that Scott's selection of passages conjures.

Times Square Red, Times Square Blue

Nevertheless, Delany was surely forced to grapple with Scott's challenge. Her essay became foundational to the emerging world of cultural studies

---

13. Scott, "Evidence of Experience," 777.
14. Ibid.

scholarship—it has been taught countless times and cited more than three thousand times, probably thanks to its vivid opening example of Delany's bathhouses—and many of the scholars Delany encountered when wearing his academic hat would certainly have known of him only through his role as the paradigm of problematic historiography according to Scott. In his third memoir, *Times Square Red, Times Square Blue*, Delany crafts a narrative that both structurally and substantively thwarts attempts to be read as taking the evidence of experience as foundational. Once again, Delany writes of sites of gay pleasure and desire, now pornographic movie theaters in Times Square instead of bathhouses in the East Village. But in this third memoir, Delany returns to the questions raised in *Heavenly Breakfast* and offers a social theory in response. The theaters, like the commune, were fleeting, but they teach a lesson about how to structure our world so that more flourishing is possible.

Times Square Red, Times Square Blue consists of two sections. The first is primarily autobiographical fragments that collectively paint a picture of the culture in and around Times Square's pornographic movie theaters. The second offers Delany's social theory meant to make sense of the world of these theaters. He writes just as the last of the theaters were being forced to close, as New York Mayor Rudolph Giuliani was "cleaning up" Times Square, preparing it for tourists. But, in prefatory remarks, Delany makes it clear that the purpose of his book is not simply to lament the passing of institutions that formed a hub of gay social life. "The polemical passion here is forward-looking, not nostalgic, however respectful it is of a past we may find useful for grounding future possibilities" (xvii-xviii). Readers might have tended to read Delany's first two memoirs as memorials to times of pleasure and freedom that have been lost, but Delany wants this book to be read as a meditation on what futures we ought to pursue. In a sense, the focus is on hope, insofar as the focus is on a possible but unlikely future possibility toward which Delany orients the reader, but hope is not a language Delany ever uses. As in his science fiction writing, in his memoirs he sketches worlds that are relatively discrete, relatively disconnected from the present, and he aims these to model futures that we are now motivated to imagine. These futures are not so much social orders governed by rules but rather spaces for people to encounter each other. And while these new spaces echo the particular gay theaters that Delany limns, he admonishes readers to imagine future spaces "available not only to gay men but to all men and women, gay and straight, over an even wider social range" than those he describes (xvii).

What Delany describes in the first section of his text is a working class–centered world of men, and the occasional woman, who would gather for intimacy, including sex, at a cluster of pornographic movie theaters. He offers vivid descriptions of these men, their practices, the theater infrastructure that supported them, the bars they gathered at when not in the theaters, and his interactions with them. The portrait he paints is one of great variety: "I've met playwrights, carpenters, opera singers, telephone repair men, stockbrokers, guys on welfare, guys with trust funds, guys on crutches . . ." (15). Delany reports that these theaters are the only places where he "had any extended conversations with some of the city's Hasidim" (16). While the media image of such theaters involves furtive visits of businessmen, in fact Delany recounts that the vast majority of the patrons were blue-collar workers. The world he depicts is far from pristine. Buildings are dilapidated, but functional; there are homeless men and men straight out of mental hospitals, but they are not a danger to others; and there are men who offer sex for money, but these are a minority.

The heart of Delany's account of the theaters is the encounters between men that happened there. While conventional wisdom sees these encounters as brief, random, and devoid of emotion, merely utilization of the bodies of others to satisfy one's own desire, Delany offers a more complicated picture of the theaters. Encounters could take a variety of forms, from brief and focused on sexual gratification to the start of long-term relationships; his interest is in the potential of each encounter. Against the image of theater patrons as men with intimacy problems avoiding the burdens of actual relationships, Delany makes the case that encounters in the theaters were actually intimate, and were actually relationships. The relatively stable population of theater patrons was generally familiar with each other, even as there were always newcomers in the theaters as well. "Intimacy for most of us is a condition that endures, however often repeated, for minutes or for hours. And these all had their intimate hours. But, like all sane relationships, they also had limits" (40). Sometimes Delany would bring back a sandwich or drink for another theater patron; sometimes he would invite one to his apartment. Sometimes they would agree, sometimes not. Sometimes, after sex, Delany would talk for hours with the other man in the theater, sometimes not at all. In such descriptions, Delany emphasizes neither a set of social norms nor pure fluidity but rather the possibility that encounters hold. To tap that possibility requires navigating one's own desire and the desire of others. In Delany's account, the vast majority of times that one theatergoer proposed sex to another, the answer was no—and this was accepted without hurt feelings.

In the second half of *Times Square Red, Times Square Blue*, Delany theorizes such encounters as a paradigm of "contact," and contact is the characteristic activity of the ideal spaces Delany imagines.[15] Contact occurs when, seemingly randomly, people from quite different backgrounds encounter each other without a transactional purpose. They may encounter each other in the line at the grocery store or post office, or on the street or at the park. The old Times Square movie theaters were particularly intense sites of contact, with so many different people encountering each other, fueled by desire—though desire for sexual gratification does not exhaust the meaning of such encounters. The possibility of contact is what gives cities their vitality, and what draws people to them. Contact makes flourishing possible. However, another feature of our world is pervasive, though often invisible, inter-class conflict. Such conflict, and particularly the interests of the wealthy, results in a limit to contact and attacks on the institutions that make contact possible (public spaces, mixed neighborhoods, pornographic theaters in Times Square). Often such attacks are made in the name of "safety"; in fact, they reduce the possibility for flourishing of all involved. (Delany does not use the term "flourishing." Rather, he writes of "pleasantness," which he describes as "pleasure in its most generalized form [though pleasure no less important or social for that]" [121].)

Delany argues that contact is also often confused with networking, but in some ways they are opposites. Networking happens at a gallery opening, a conference, or a gym. People of the same class, with similar interests, gather in order to advance those interests. Networking promises short-term rewards (new opportunities, new business, more money), but in fact it rarely yields the rewards it promises. Since everyone gathered for networking is looking for the same rewards, and there are not enough to be shared, most will go away materially disappointed. What is useful about networking is the knowledge that can be exchanged quickly about issues of common concern, and so can smooth and stabilize a career path—but rarely does it result in the hoped-for book deal, mentoring relationship, or job opportunity. In contrast, Delany offers many examples of contact

---

15. As Delany points out, this method itself fosters a sort of contact, between vernacular and expert discourses.

yielding material benefits, from a vacuum cleaner acquired at a copy center to job connections made at pornographic theaters. At the end of the day, Delany concedes, there is a good deal of overlap between contact and networking—they are, in his argument, ideal types—but thematizing the distinction can guide the way we arrange our lives, individually and collectively.

Contact is not the same thing as community, Delany makes clear. Community suggests norms, values, histories, and boundaries. Contact suggests a site of encounter. Certain characteristics may develop around a site of contact, but they are secondary to the encounters, and the characteristics can change as the encounters change, as the human-to-human interactions change. Making the difference between contact and community explicit distinguishes Delany's third memoir from his first two. Each of those earlier works could be read as laments for communities lost, whereas Delany is very clear in *Times Square Red, Times Square Blue* that his intention is to find evidence from the past of a social structure that maximizes human flourishing so that it can be pursued in the future. Finding this evidence requires depicting the texture of a community, but what such descriptions are really doing is depicting the site of contact that makes the community possible. At the same time, the specific events that occasioned the writing of *Times Square Red, Times Square Blue* should not be forgotten. Wealthy investors and their partners in city government were conspiring to transform Times Square into a tourist destination, complete with Disney Store and plenty of police. Delany's project is not only to name a zone of contact but also to name the forces that attempt to stamp it out, that aspire to class homogeneity.

Delany, a Different Kind of Prophet

Here we have Samuel R. Delany, prophet. He is at once vehemently condemning worldly forces that would prevent human flourishing and also promising a future of pleasure and pleasantness, of flourishing, if his advice is heeded. Perhaps this was the implicit stance of Delany's two earlier memoirs, but it becomes crystal-clear in his third. Yet despite this prophetic form, *Times Square Red, Times Square Blue* is not structured by hope (nor by nostalgia). The narrative pragmatically sketches scenes from the past in order to remind readers about what a future might involve. There is no clear path from here to there, from our present moment to the future where all will flourish. There is also no specific content to that flourishing in the future, no specific practices, norms, or institutions that will fill the world. In this way, Delany's narrative resists hope, for there are not particular objects onto which hope can fix itself. There is, at most, a mood or atmosphere of pleasantness (which "hangs in the street" when there is contact, Delany evocatively writes [183]). And there are fragments from the past that can be repeated differently, fragments that give us a feel for the pleasantness that Delany promises but that are themselves forever gone, even as they motivate us to imagine anew.

There is a certain strand of critical theory that appeals to an abstract notion of undefined future possibility to animate engagement in the complexities of the present. Such accounts often draw on the work of Walter Benjamin to imagine a spirit of "messianism," a sense that at some unknown point the radically other will break into the world, revealing the contingency and injustice of our world. In such accounts, it is crucial to limit the content of such messianism: the interruption that we anticipate can only be described as an interruption; it is inscrutable from the vantage point of the present, for if it were otherwise, the interruption would not be so complete. Historically-oriented scholars have used such a framework to guide their narratives, pointing to moments when radically new ways of organizing the world flickered, then were stamped out—with the scholar's job not to monumentalize such moments but to use them as inspiration, motivating and legitimizing experiments in thinking and living radically otherwise today.[16]

At first, this sounds like Delany's project in *Times Square Red, Times Square Blue*—but if this messianic framework resonates with Delany's work, it would be with *Heavenly Breakfast*. By his third memoir, Delany emphasizes the social forces that block spaces of flourishing (a project of ideology critique shared by some Benjaminian critics) and also fills in what is most essential about those spaces of flourishing. Here Delany is not rigorously apophatic. The spaces he admires and desires are not wholly other than the world, illegible from the perspective of current discourse. They are already present in our world, in public spaces: parks, squares, markets, and the like. But even more importantly, they are characterized by a certain mode of interaction, potential-filled encounters, even as Delany is apophatic about

---

16. See especially Wilder, *Freedom Time*; also, for reading strategies that suggest historical figures' commitment to messianism, Smith, *Weird John Brown*; Lambelet, *¡Presente!*

the particular contours and shades of any future world so characterized. In other words, Delany offers guidance and constraints on the sort of futures that we ought to be imagining. They ought to have the architecture, in the broadest sense, to support contact, but they also ought not look at all like the world we have now, riven with inter-class conflict. To imagine those futures of flourishing, Delany refuses analytical prose. He writes in aestheticized fragments from the past—and, of course, he also writes science fiction.

Another theoretical idiom that approaches Delany's project is that of the civic republican tradition that claims freedom is best understood as non-domination. The paradigm, here, is slave and master: freedom means having no masters, having no one with power to arbitrarily exercise their will over you. In our contemporary world, domination conceals itself in structures, but the underlying dynamic is the same—whether it is gender domination (patriarchy), racial domination (white supremacy), economic domination (capitalism), or any other form. Freedom will come when these systems are dismantled, in this view. For Delany, flourishing will come when humans can encounter each other in zones of contact uncontaminated by economic domination (which, we might generously suggest, stands in for all forms of domination).[17] For kataphatic civic republicans, political theorists can draw up lists of institutions and best practices for creating contexts free of domination.[18] For apophatic civic republicans, political theorists are tasked with enumerating forms of domination and gesturing in the direction of a future without domination.[19] Delany offers a middle path, suggesting the sorts of institutions and best practices that could mitigate domination while also resisting the urge to fill in the precise features of a world without domination.[20]

---

17. In Delany's memoirs, zones of contact, free of economic domination, are necessarily (if rather implausibly) free of racial and gender domination as well—presumably through something like the power of a truly human encounter. He tells of how he brought a female friend to the pornographic theaters in the old Times Square and she was fully accepted and came to feel comfortable there.

18. Pettit, *Republicanism*.

19. Roberts attributes this view to Marx in *Marx's Inferno*.

20. But is republicanism, understood as non-domination, the same as democracy? I think so, but I realize this is a controversial view. Once kings, masters, and bosses are eliminated, the people govern themselves. As long as new forces of domination are held at bay, the people will develop the practices and institutions for self-governance—practices and institutions that cannot be theorized from the perspective of the present. In this I follow James et al., *Facing Reality*.

Delany employs a secular idiom in his memoirs, even as he toys with religious idioms in his science fiction writings.[21] But the structure of his prophecy, if we are to call it that, could be expressed in a more theological idiom. What he condemns are worldly interests that would make themselves gods: the real estate and political interests that are transforming Times Square, in particular, but all forces of domination more generally. What he commends is rightly-oriented desire. Once domination is suspended, once worldly masters are set aside, we encounter each other and each other's desire, and we learn the pleasure that comes in and from negotiating desires. "I learned to move within the circle of other people's desire, and be at ease as I generated my own. And I would strike one of my senses before I would part with that knowledge," he reflects in *Heavenly Breakfast* (20). Moreover, Delany imagines something like a life of ultimate happiness ("pleasantness"), but he acknowledges that in our world it is inaccessible. Contact and networking are always entangled in our world, and that means domination (the hierarchical contexts in which networking takes place) always contaminates potential sites of freedom. Yet attending to stories of contact from the past fuels our belief that contact—ultimate happiness—may be possible in the future, even if there is not sufficient evidence to support that belief. In other words, Delany's storytelling models a narrative of faith: not faith that grows out of comfort in community but faith that grows out of comfort glimpsed and lost, and, perhaps, obtainable again.[22]

Does it make sense to call Samuel R. Delany a secular prophet? Or a prophetic critic? Perhaps these two terms, prophet and prophetic critic, should not be used interchangeably. The auspicious term "prophet" suggests a desire to speak to the world, whether or not the world will listen. (The world ignores the prophet at its peril.) Michael Walzer suggests that prophetic criticism is part of democratic life, an activity that we all engage in as we reflect on the values of our community (whether it is our household, our neighborhood, or our nation) and as we call out the mismatch of current practices to those values.[23] While there may be some individuals who carry out prophetic criticism on a grand scale, like Martin Luther King, Walzer calls us to recognize the ordinariness of prophetic activity.

21. Scott, "Delany's Divinities."

22. Why faith and not hope? To follow Augustine, hope is about the possibility of goodness in the future while faith involves beliefs about the good and the bad, in the past, present, and future. The emphasis in Delany, as explicated here, is on the latter.

23. Walzer, *Interpretation and Social Criticism.*

The Prophet Samuel R. Delany

Neither of these terms quite fits Delany, and yet there does seem to be a prophetic-like quality to some of his writing. Moreover, the form of prophetic-like writing that Delany produces resonates with justice-seeking social movements today. Not only in his project of imagining futures through science fiction, but also in his attempts to imagine futures through analysis of fragments of the past in his memoirs. These imaginings center human encounter, challenge systems of domination, and orient a desire for a better future without leaning on hope (so frequently conflated with optimism). In other words, it seems that Delany stretches the way we think prophecy, forces us to think the prophet and prophetic criticism anew in ways that we do not yet have the vocabulary to represent.

But does Delany really fit in a social movement context, let alone a racial justice movement context? While he is a Black American, and he occasionally writes about race, it is not a primary feature of his analytical or literary writing. And while he moves in broadly leftist spaces (a commune in the '60s, the New York gay scene later), he does not do so as a social movement participant. Perhaps it is precisely this location that a prophetic figure must take in an era where prophetic figures fall under suspicion. In a leaderful rather than leaderless movement, prophets are perhaps to be found on the margins of a movement rather than at the center. Even the most democratically-oriented prophetic figures who find themselves at the center of movements are vulnerable to criticism from within and beyond a movement. Consider, for example, Paul Robeson, another polymath who confounded attempts to confine Black excellence to a single lane.[24] Robeson was a star athlete, a lawyer, an activist, a singer, and a movie star—until his career came crashing down due to McCarthy-era accusations of Communist affiliation. Robeson was committed to using his platform, as he sang freedom songs and prophesied a new political order, to catalyze social movements. He did that, but he also saw his position undermined and his mental and physical health destroyed in the process. Perhaps we can learn from Delany that the prophet, like the sites of contact of which he writes, exists only momentarily, at the edges, fugitive—and ultimately in our imaginations. But that work of imagining is crucial, fueling commitment to struggles in the present that illuminates a future of happiness.

Delany is a prophet suited for here and now, the US in the early twenty-first century, grappling with the meaning of racial justice after three decades of multiculturalism led to a Black president but also to

---

24. See especially Redmond, *Everything Man*.

the deaths of Trayvon Martin and Michael Brown, not to racial justice. It led to the realization that democracy when racial domination, or any domination, persists is not genuine democracy. That ultimately impotent era of multiculturalism fetishized the Black prophet, Martin Luther King and those in his mold. Rather than looking for new prophets in the old mold to lead us to the promised land, we can now realize that there was a fundamental confusion in how we thought about prophecy. With the help of Delany's model, we can look for other prophets, writ large and writ small, though always at the edges—not only today but in the past as well, and still to be born.

7

Secular Prophecy and the Name of God

Tom James

OTHER ESSAYS IN THIS volume well demonstrate that prophecy has a life outside the domain of churches and other religious communities. Indeed, one may go further and argue that some of the most fertile sources of prophecy lay precisely beyond the confines of religious institutions: precisely, that is, within the secular. Prophecy, we might say, is inherently anti-clerical, or at least anti-sacerdotal. Religions build temples. Prophets rail against them. And so it should be no surprise to find that the prophetic edge of human experience, seeing "a way out of no way,"[1] critiquing unjust social structures, etc., has been more consistently and more radically developed as a social practice in the secular arena than in the institutionalized religious sphere, which has often been all too entrenched in the present order of things to welcome prophecy. In terms of the wider concern of this book, one wonders whether prophecy functions and is more clearly identified in the humanities than in theology.

On the other hand, thinkers from Paul Tillich to Walter Brueggemann to Wilda Gafney[2] have found the prophetic at the heart of biblical religion.

---

1. Coleman argues that this phrase, based on Isaiah 43:19, describes the praxis of black women in the United States in their struggles against racism and sexism. See Coleman, *Making a Way Out of No Way*, 33.

2. See Tillich, *Biblical Religion and the Search for Ultimate Reality*, 1–4; Brueggemann, *Prophetic Imagination*, 21–38; Gafney, *Daughters of Miriam*, 151–64.

Prophets speak for a God who liberated slaves, according to the founding myth of Israel. As Norman Gottwald has argued in his book, *The Tribes of Yahweh*, this liberating God was known more immediately as the one who empowered the struggles of the rural tribes that would eventually become Israel against the ruling elites of urban kingdoms in Canaan.[3] In the Hebrew Scriptures, the very name of God is tied to a desire and a demand for liberation. So, given both the resistance of institutionalized religion to prophecy, on the one hand, and the fundamental role of prophecy within biblical religion, on the other, how do we interpret the relationship between prophetic speech and action, struggling against the *status quo*, and explicit talk about God that is the focus of institutionalized monotheism and its theologies? In this chapter, I want to frame the question somewhat more narrowly: Does prophecy in the name of God have anything distinctive to say, anything to teach us? Or is it, at best, a bit of imagery or a well of motivation, cluing us in to obligations and opportunities that are better grasped by public reason or critical social analysis, or simply by participation in struggle? Another way to ask the same question is, Does prophetic speech and action that is rooted in a theological vision have anything to add to what Robin D. G. Kelley has called the "new knowledge"[4] that comes when we dare to fight for or simply imagine social change?

The key issue here, as in so many similar questions, is the status of claims about transcendence. Does prophecy have a transcendent source or reference point, and, if so, is theology specially fitted to talk about it? As we have seen in these essays, the latter hardly flows automatically from the former: who is to say that transcendence isn't best accounted for by those outside traditional religious institutions?

Broadly speaking, there are two poles that tend to frame the options. First, some have argued for what we may describe as a "hard" insistence on divine revelation or what I will call a "theological anti-secularism." True knowledge of God and ourselves, advocates claim, is only available through some kind of revelatory event or source. All claims to prophecy that fall outside this remit would then be regarded as illusory, or, as Barth put it, as further episodes in humanity's dialogue with itself.[5] Prophecy, in this view (or, I should say, *true* prophecy), falls strictly in the theological domain. All the rest is either illusion or, at best, vaguely analogous to the genuine

---

3. Gottwald, *Tribes of Yahweh*, 489–93.
4. Kelley, *Freedom Dreams*, 8.
5. Barth, *Church Dogmatics* I/1, 20–21.

article. The opposite view, that I will call "prophetic secularism" but could also be called "secular prophecy," is that knowledge of what is most important both factually and morally is sourced fully immanently, so that any role for revelation would be illustrative or perhaps motivational but not really informative. In this view, it would be something like secular reason (or, once again, critical social analysis) that does all the heavy lifting. Religion doesn't provide special knowledge or insight and so prophecy would be open to anyone who is able to mine the contradictions of their society and/or to announce a path forward, whether in searching prose or in fiery poetry, or anywhere in between.

There have been middle paths of numerous kinds to these rather extreme and wooden alternatives. The purpose of these essay is to develop one such possibility with respect to prophecy. Drawing on Paul Tillich and John Caputo, with an assist from political theorist Jodi Dean, I argue that the prophetic task of theology is vigilantly to guard against the closure or ossification of imaginaries of governance and transformation. I am attempting to revive what has been called, following Tillich, a "theology of culture": mining the vectors within our many complex cultures today that point to some ultimate loyalty or confidence and then subjecting those vectors to scrutiny. Do they open us toward continual transformation, teaching us to ask searching critical questions about ourselves and to refuse easy, conventional resolutions? Or do they, on the other hand, close thinking down around a preferred set of values or assumptions or modes of interpretation, teaching us to rest secure in some pattern of meaning or some particular orientation toward the world?

It is important to see that one may plausibly attribute a "prophetic" sensibility or mindset to either. Classically, the "liberal" approaches to culture of a nineteenth century that regarded European (read "white") civilizations as the definitive world leaders in an inevitable march toward a simultaneously more humane and technologically advanced society were deeply motivated by what we may call a kind of prophecy. But the problem, which appears obvious to us today, is that they closed down the meaning of the transcendent edge of human experience that unsettles complacencies, etc., identifying it all too completely with the leading edge of European (white) civilization. Simply put, the word "God" was affixed to the "civilizing" mission of the West. More recently, and in some ways with the opposite political intention, emancipatory projects focused on the liberation of oppressed non-white groups have likewise mobilized prophetic expectations. And they, too, recognize a specific historical protagonist as bearer of the transcendent edge or the opening of history. In this case, the heroes of the story are those who are on history's "underside," those whose underclass position in the global network of money and power make them suitable bearers of a word of divine condemnation. As different as these two examples are, both projects are prophetic in that they mine contradictions with modern societies and propose a sort of vanguard that may lead us toward a more humane and better world order. But there is a danger from the point of theological prophecy that attends both in precisely the same way. Each is in danger of closing down the force of the unconditioned, of closing ourselves off from the call of the transcendent edge of prophecy which relentlessly destabilizes configurations of value and meaning and thus consistently assaults us with demands for self-reflection—or, in religiously terms, calls for repentance.[6]

This is not to suggest an equivalence between the ongoing projects of white supremacy and cultural chauvinism on the one hand and emancipatory movements of the oppressed on the other. As Reinhold Niebuhr once argued, prophecy that flattens in this way is literally of no worldly use since it undermines any method we might have of making relative judgments about the values of very different social and political projects.[7] Moreover, as I will argue later in the essay, emancipatory projects have a special affinity if not outright identification with the aims of theological prophecy. It is to insist, however, on the fundamental meaning of transcendence. Before God, if there is no equivalence, there is at least a kind of solidarity in weakness, a common fragility or even danger that lurks within any system of thought that identifies rogues and heroes within history. The specific danger here is the possibility of what we might call "reigns of terror" in which legitimate claims of the oppressed against their oppressors are absolutized so that the latter lose their standing as human beings with claims of their own to make. The role of theological prophecy or prophetic theology, I will argue, is not to side with either the oppressed or the oppressor in an *absolute* fashion (though, I will argue, it must side with the oppressed in a *relative* fashion) but to unsettle any kind of absolutization at all. To borrow

---

6. At best, this danger generates a conversational dynamic of continual challenge and critique. See, for example, the introduction, entitled "Expanding the View," to Gutiérrez, *Theology of Liberation*, xvii–xlvi.

7. See, for example, Niebuhr's 1957 essay "Why Is Barth Silent on Hungary?," 183–90.

a metaphor from Tillich, theological prophecy shakes foundations[8]—it does not build them. Foundations, whether they be centuries-old orders of oppression or revolutionary re-orderings of society, are always human constructions (albeit in concert with many non-human but still creaturely factors like climate, geography, disease, etc.), and therefore the work of theological prophecy must be to keep those foundations susceptible to shaking, which is another way of saying that theological prophecy aims above all things to underscore the incompleteness of any historical mission.

This brings us to what we might call the "radical" prophetic option: what I am calling "theological anti-secularism." According to this view, the "secular" prophecies embedded with human experience and its cultural reflections are always false because they collapse the basic distinction between God and cultural projects. As will become clear, I reject this view, and yet the vivid distinction it draws between theological (true) prophecy and (false) secular prophecy demands attention.

Theological Anti-secularism: Secular Prophecy Is Always False

Theological anti-secularism is not new but may be thought of as a perennial option in the church. Famously, Tertullian asked, "What has Athens to do with Jerusalem?" What, in other words, can the authority of even the "best" of human culture have legitimately to say in the hearing of divine revelation? The towering representative of theological anti-secularism in the modern thought is twentieth-century Protestant theologian Karl Barth. Here it must be made clear that "anti-secularism" does not mean that the world is despised or even that human thought about the world is useless. Barth was deeply engaged in fierce criticism of social injustice and just as seriously invested in reform. Moreover, he fully accepted the prerogative of natural and social sciences to pursue rational methods in describing and analyzing the world, and also of literature and art to depict truths about human experience. His theological anti-secularism lay, rather, in his stark distinction between such secular pursuits which had, in his judgment, the power to account for what he called the "phenomena" of human experience, and the claims of theology, which, he judged, pertain to the deepest realities of life, or to what we might call "ultimacy" or the "unconditional."

What accounts for the distinction, or rather, with the radical way in which it is drawn? For Barth, the force of the distinction rests in the claim

---

8. Tillich, *Shaking of the Foundations*, 1–11.

that humanity has been spoken to. Divine revelation tells the truth about our lives because it speaks from God's perspective, and only God's perspective penetrates the fog of human self-deception. All human thought, scientific rigor, creativity, etc., amounts by comparison to a vast and protracted dialogue of humanity with itself. The dialogue is illuminating, and deeply interesting, but, in a crucial way it is false. We tell false stories about ourselves because of our all too human desire for self-justification. Barth argues that what may look like an internal psychological defensiveness, however, is in fact a pervasive feature of human experience that generates historic catastrophes. In his own time, the screaming example was the horrors of Nazism, which he interpreted as exactly what happens when a nation believes in its own virtue and when such misguided belief is supported by the church—when, in other words, the prophetic word is collapsed into a nation's own self-understanding. But this catastrophe is taken as paradigmatic of the human condition more generally: humanity's dialogue with itself elides the voice of God and is consequently lost in sin and destruction.[9] James Cone, a founding figure of black theology, developed this line of thought in his early writings, identifying Barth's dialogue of humanity with itself as the complacency and self-justification of whiteness. For Cone, the deceptions of the world, its lostness in sin, are expressed in its valorization and defense of white supremacy.[10]

Cone's use of this Barthian theme suggests that theological prophecy need not be indifference to the world but can be opposition to the world or to its dominant structures. In the partially completed Part Four of Volume Four on his *Church Dogmatics*, Barth wrote of the "lordless powers" that dominate human civilizations, creating various kinds of disorders and disruptions.[11] However, Barth does not valorize order as such—very far from it. Instead, following the Augustinian tradition, he argues for a true or good order that embodies justice and humaneness. "Power as such," he had written in an earlier volume, is "evil." That is, power that is not governed by the good—more specifically, by God's gracious election of humanity as

---

9. These themes are evident throughout the broad sweep of Barth's work, though ring most loudly in his earlier writings. See, for example, Barth, *Word of God and the Word of Man*, 9–27.

10. Cone, *Black Theology and Black Power*, 61–80. See also Lloyd, *Religion of the Field Negro*, 21–38. Lloyd argues that there is a deep connection between whiteness as Cone describes it and secularism.

11. Barth, *Christian Life*, 213–33.

God's partner—is antithetical to the gospel.[12] The "lordless powers" are the powers of nationalism, capitalist accumulation, and militarism that undermine connections and solidarities between peoples and generate social and moral chaos. But the lordless powers are not directly anarchic—instead, they promote orders in the form of states and institutions that defect from or distort the true or good order characteristic of God's creation. Therefore, Christian faithfulness in the face of these powers is revolt against the false orders which are really dis-orders: as he paradoxically puts it, the Christian life is a "revolt against disorder."[13]

Theological or true prophecy, in this view, is a word that can speak to the condition of sin: it is a word of resistance and revolt. Only a word from the beyond can disrupt our ruinous self-satisfaction and complacency and, in addition, strike a blow against the kind of hubris that ruthlessly implements the terms of its utopian experiments. For the young Barth, the prophetic therefore had a bolt from the blue character: it strikes in a word of judgment and a call to repentance without warning, because to be able to apprehend a warning would be to anticipate the prophetic word and therefore in some respect to be able to reproduce it. A rigorous theological anti-secularism must resist this framing because it allows us to think of the prophetic word as our own word, an elevated but still all too enclosed dialogue of humanity with itself.

Barth's approach, as I say, demands attention. It offers a striking way of accounting for the radical, unsettling character of biblical prophecy. As will become clear, I wish to preserve this unsettling feature as essential to the meaning and function of theological prophecy (or prophetic theology). Before I give reasons for being unsatisfied with theological anti-secularism as an approach, however, I must report that, unfortunately, its contemporary expressions have significantly declined from its high-water mark in Barth. Stanley Hauerwas, who was anointed America's best theologian by Time Magazine in 2001, has domesticated Barth's word of prophecy within the confines of the church. For Hauerwas, truth is in the distinctive stories and peaceable practices borne by the church in its contrast with the false stories and violent practices that characterize the secular world.[14] John Milbank, pioneer of school of thought that calls itself "radical orthodoxy," has

---

12. Barth, *Church Dogmatics* II/1, 524.

13. Barth, *Church Dogmatics* IV/4, 205–13.

14. See for example, Hauerwas's influential antiwar book, *Against the Nations: War and Survival in a Liberal Society*.

followed Hauerwas more than Barth in identifying theological truth not with an unsettling event that shakes us from our complacencies but with a set of metaphysical claims borne by church tradition; though in his case, these claims would assert themselves as a better public reason, thus underwriting a return to a culture dominated by theology and the church.[15] By being anti-secular, Hauerwas and Milbank seek to be more authentically or faithfully Christian. But, though they retain a healthily polemic attitude toward the wider world, they lose the prophetic spirit which is turned not simply against secular culture but against the church as well. All the secularity of the prophetic—its resistance to sacred structure and inviolable tradition, its tendency to rail against temples—is lost.

But the basic problem with theological anti-secularism is deeper than the shortcomings of its contemporary expressions. The problem is fundamental to the approach itself. Despite his radicalism, Barth himself fell prey at times to a stultifying otherworldliness. When the Soviet Union invaded Hungary in 1956 to crush political dissent that was driven by worker activism and democratic aspirations, Barth remained silent, seeming to adopt a studied neutrality. What happened, we might ask, to the revolt against disorder? What was at issue was not humility before historical complexity but a way of approaching theological truth claims. Since every social and political system, every secular ordering of human life, embodies a broken and sinful humanity aiming at its self-justification, it is difficult if not impossible to leverage the prophetic distinction between God and the idols to support particular social and political movements or demands. To be somewhat more precise, this kind of theological prophecy is able to expose pretentions and idolatries, and therefore to mobilize critique and resistance, but it has a much harder time taking sides or positively supporting revolutionary or even reformist movements for change. And, so, the democratic demands emerging from political movements in the satellite states of the Soviet regime, for example, are no more pressing than any other moral or social demand.[16] Simply put, the prophetic here is defined by a distance from burning historical issues, issues of life and death. Earlier, I referenced Reinhold Niebuhr's critique of Barth precisely on this refusal

---

15. Milbank's most important work is *Theology and Social Theory: Beyond Secular Reason*.

16. Never one to bow to pressure, Barth responded to Niebuhr's criticism of his silence with the following: "I ask why Niebuhr is silent about American prisons. Wouldn't it be wiser if he thought of things nearer to him than farther away? When he speaks out on this, I will speak out on Hungary." See Barth, *Barth in Conversation*, 116.

of judgment.[17] It is a strange version of the prophetic, we might agree, that refuses to take sides, to take wings and fly, as Niebuhr sarcastically charged, remaining thousands of feet about the very conflicts that cry out for prophecy.

It is important to see that this is not simply a matter of getting it right about historical geopolitical conflicts. By the logic of a theological anti-secularism (the strictures of which, thankfully, Barth did not always adhere), we would also have no reason to stand with, say, national liberation movements against US hegemony or with domestic movements for freedom and equality within racist, sexist, capitalist societies today. If the prophetic word comes only from the beyond, if it levels all distinctions between strong and weak, oppressor and oppressed, then, while structures of oppression may be critiqued as "lordless powers," relative judgements about worse and better alternatives are undermined. More seriously, the oppressed themselves are denied the right and the capacity to bear the prophetic word of annunciation: their demands for democracy, for example, find no specific theological support.

The one exception to this rule proves its force. Barth's theology arose out of a specific kind of social conflict: the claims of the state and the wider European culture it grew out of against the church's claims for autonomy. The young Barth was famously horrified by the sight of his theology professors unanimously supporting Germany's aggressive posture leading up to the first World War and the assumptions of cultural and natural superiority that their support suggested. Later, he was deeply involved in the German church's resistance to being subjected to the direct authority of the Nazi state. Barth was a principal author of the 1934 Barmen Declaration, which reads like the cry of protest of an oppressed people. Importantly, however, the claim being made by the "confessing churches" who backed the Declaration was not that their experience of oppression exposed a flaw within society that needed correction. It was only that they were compelled by their faith to take up a disobedient posture toward the state because the state was asking them to submit to an alien (i.e., as secular) authority. Although their stance was strong and courageous, the prophetic is circumscribed in their response in terms of both its authorization and its content. It is authorized only for the specific community who is oriented to hear the divine Word: the church. Its content is narrowed to the finest point, expressing its exclusive loyalty to God (or, for Barth, God as revealed in Jesus Christ). It

---

17. Niebuhr, "Why Is Barth Silent on Hungary?," 183–90.

therefore offers, at best, only an indirect word of condemnation of Nazism. Just as importantly, there is no word of annunciation on behalf of a better social order beyond the boundaries of the church.

Prophetic Secularism: All Prophecy Is Secular Prophecy

I have already critiqued what I am calling "prophetic secularism" in the introductory paragraphs of this chapter, so there is no need to prolong the analysis. I will simply make one historical reference and suggest two particular ways that prophetic secularism plays out in contemporary US society.

First, the historical reference. The view that all prophecy is secular prophecy can take many distinct forms, depending on what one takes prophecy to be and how one understands the secular. But the prototypical case, though it is complicated, is surely Immanuel Kant. In *Religion within the Limits of Reason Alone* (1793), Kant argued that all of what is important to know for living one's life can be discerned on the basis of what he called "pure practical reason"—practical because concerned with questions of human action and "pure" because unadulterated with the trappings of tradition, historical loyalties, etc. Religion, in this view, serves not to inform or to guide but to illustrate or to motivate. If one thinks of the prophetic as operating only in the affective register, then prophecy would fall to religion as the spur that persuades us to moral action. But prophecy in biblical tradition isn't, of course, purely a motivator: its principal vocation is to expose truth. For the Kantian line, however, truth is discerned by a public, secular reason alone, so the interesting features of prophecy fall to the side of the secular.

So much for the historical reference. The more pressing issue is how prophetic secularism is expressed in contemporary cultures and societies. The most enduring form, if notoriously difficult to pin down, is modern liberalism. The general procedure by means of which liberalism discerns truth about societies is appeal to a publicly shared discourse governed by rational principles. Of course, liberalism has been from the beginning an emancipatory project: deciding truth on the basis of appeals to reason has been a way to support individual autonomy vis-à-vis the state and tradition. There is a distinctive kind of prophecy that operates within this register: the prophetic for modern liberalism is the leading edge of the process of rational consensus-reaching that furthers individual freedom. Liberalism as prophecy denounces or condemns that which lags behind while confident that, since it is grounded in shared secular reason, the victory of correct opinions and, with them, humane and just practices, is inevitable.

What liberalism seems constitutionally unable to grasp, however, is that this shared consensus is shot through with numerous contradictions and conflicts. What emerges as rational consensus is inevitably tinged with assumptions that reflect the privileged positions of capitalists and conquerors. The prophecy of liberalism both denounces the past and announces a better future in the name of cultural vanguards who enjoy positions of relative power and authority. Historically, if we are being honest, progress was identified with the expansion of whiteness: white experiences became normative human experiences; while values became universal values; white skin became the standard of beauty, trustworthiness, humanity. Liberalism is a prophecy of whiteness overcoming internal and external barbarisms. As many critics have pointed out, there is a deep connection between the liberal project and colonialism. But, on the other hand, it is not as if everyone in the "center" countries is invested equally in this process. It is more specifically embedded in relatively privileged class positions, especially in what often goes by the name of the "professional managerial class," a class specializing in the use of rational principles and confident in their power to order societies properly. This yields a prophecy that is ordered not toward fundamental transformation of societies but toward a reformism that seeks precisely to preserve the basic elements and power relationships characteristic of white society through a series of adjustments and compromises. The prophetic itself therefore suffers a diminution of its power and scope. Liberal reformism is a prophecy drained of prophetic juice.

But liberalism is far from the only secular prophecy or prophetic secularism. There is also what I will call the "secularism of the left." Here I have mind the prophetic orientation of radical social movements, including both the "old left" of socialist and labor activism and the broader "new left" struggles against colonialism, patriarchy, anti-blackness, heteronormativity, etc.[18] The secularism of the left is distinguished from liberalism by its break with reformism and from an orientation toward the perspective of a white professional managerial class. It is accordingly less focused on public reason and universal criteria of judgment than on critical social analysis.

---

18. This division, while roughly accurate historically speaking, is conceptually problematic, since the "old left" was always feminist and multi-racial, despite its difficulties with both race and gender, while the "new left" was equally invested in anti-capitalist agitation. Today, one hopes that we are witnessing a kind of productive merger of the two tendencies, though there is much work to be done.

The latter is the principal source of the secularism of the left's prophecy both in terms of denunciation of the present order and annunciation of utopian possibility. As we will see in the next section, much of the flavor as well as the content of this approach corresponds to how I will describe theological prophecy. Both are oriented toward fundamental transformations of the social order and both are critically rooted in deep suspicion of dominant forms of rationality, suspecting that rational consensus is really the consensus of the ruling class, imposed on wider societies as ideology.

What is lacking from the secularism of the left, and from prophetic secularism more generally, is the kind of reservation that can prevent fanaticism. When social analysis simply subsumes the prophetic, we become susceptible to demonic furies because we fail to attend to the incompleteness of history: we fail to keep the openness of human experience open. This failure is expressed in a dilemma perennially experienced by the left. On the one hand, leftists may choose to give themselves over to a series of balkanized struggles but find themselves unable to find a way to transcend the parameters of their specific aims in order to develop broad solidarities that could possibly mobilize democratic majorities for change. Or, on the other hand, they may adopt the pretense of universal redemption narratives that make them unable to see their own incompleteness and spur them to police their orthodoxies with all the self-righteous fury of, well, the police. In either case, the failure or the blockage occurs because the secularism of the left tends to get trapped within a purely immanent frame: it fails to discern the opening of transcendence that unsettles its own achievements.

Nevertheless, the importance of what prophetic secularism achieves cannot be denied. Though it is never as universalizing as it pretends to be, the emancipatory thrust of the trajectory of Enlightenment in western cultures, both in its liberal and radical forms, has given aid to movements of peoples who have claim their rights and their dignity, and who have dared to imagine that, as a left slogan puts it, "another world is possible."

The Name of God and Theological Prophecy (or Prophetic Theology)

The problematic with which the brief analyses in this chapter so far leave us is: can we find a form of prophecy that attends to the perpetual incompleteness of social formations and human aims (as in theological anti-secularism) while also being able to take up and interpret the contradictions

Secular Prophecy and the Name of God

within our societies and to support mobilizations, organizations, and judgments that take seriously the demands of what we might call "relative justice?" In the rest of this essay I argue that it is precisely this problematic that a *theological* prophecy or a prophetic theology, with its attention to what I will call "the name of God," sets out to address. I will not argue that, without theology, we are doomed to some kind of demonic fury. I will argue, however, that prophetic theology is oriented toward to attending to precisely this problem.

But we should remember the temptation and the prophetic failure of Barth. If there is to be a distinctively theological type of prophecy that can actually guide human agency rather than issue blanket condemnations of any and all human pretense, two things are required. First, we must be able to identify some datum that theological discourse attends and interprets. There must, in other words, be an identifiable trace of transcendence in the world: though we cannot see God (a seen god would be an idol), we would need to be able to identify traces of God, lacunae in the fabric of history that suggest openings to differing possibilities. Clearly, this requirement distances such a project from theological anti-secularism, which mistrusts if not condemns all such expression as false and dangerous. Barth refused to see, for example, movements toward democratization or liberation as suggestions of divine interruption.

But a second requirement is that some mechanism must be established to prevent expressions of transcendence from closing in upon themselves. The opening must be kept open; history, progress, transformation, reform and revolution must be viewed always as incomplete. Following the lead of philosopher-theologian John Caputo, I suggest that one such powerful mechanism is what he calls "the name of God." The name of God is a linguistic construct, a stock-in-trade of theology—in fact, the name of God is *the* stock-in-trade, the one tool that gives theology both its blessing and its curse, its distinctive logic and its relentless succession of problems. I will argue in the final section of this chapter, again following Caputo's urging, that the name of God is infinitely translatable: the reality to which it refers may be characterized in an endless succession of ways. What is ultimately important is not the name, that very particular linguistic construct over which theology obsesses and must obsess, but that which stirs within the name. Another way of saying this is to say that the name of God does not capture transcendence—if it did, transcendence would no longer transcend. The name of God cannot be God: it bears the holy but cannot *be* the holy. Nevertheless, it does function in a peculiar way which gives theological prophecy its theological character and offers something distinctive to prophecy in general. As Gordon Kaufman once argued, the word "God" functions in the discourses of western (monotheistic) religious traditions to resist idolatry: it relativizes any configuration of value and meaning which would claim to be ultimate, including belief in God itself along with any associated list of doctrines.[19]

We may note at this point, by way of initial assessment, that a theology of culture, equipped both with the name of God and with some datum or set of data to interpret that allows it (provisionally) to identify operations of transcendence in the world, seeks a middle path between theological anti-secularism and prophetic secularism, both identifying transcendence as an "edge" or an "opening" that functions within culture and vigilantly guarding the transcendence of that edge or the openness of that opening.

Perhaps the most difficult question for a theology of culture focused on the prophetic is: What is it that is visible within our cultures—our political movements, our literatures, our speech—that can serve as an indicator of the operation of transcendence? What can we confidently identify as a divine interruption? I should be careful to underscore once again that it is not that we can identify the divine reality itself, but rather than we need to be able to identify traces of God or transcendence—*loci* within history where it is opened to an alternative trajectory or possibility. Or, to borrow from Derrida, we need to be able to see where the closures of the world fail, where a whole or a pattern is built around the inclusion of some external reality that cannot be fully incorporated. Throughout the rest of this essay, I propose that this edge or trace, this opening toward alternative futures, is visible as the work of desire.

Desire has a peculiar, prophetic structure. It is embedded in culture, keenly felt and vividly expressed, fully immanent and woven into the push and pull of bodies and histories in conflict, and yet it refuses enclosure within any configuration of meaning and value that is inscribed within culture. The work of desire that is visible in various cultural expressions presses beyond itself. While particular desires may achieve specific satisfactions, desire is structurally restless—it relentlessly pushes beyond any satisfaction, susceptible to being rekindled at each stage or moment of any historical trajectory. It is the restlessness of desire that suggests its

---

19. Kaufman, *In Face of Mystery*, 301–20.

affiliation with transcendence. In this respect, we may say that desire is fully within, but not entirely of, the world.

It is important to think of desire not as an abstract wanting of who-knows-what, but to see it in its fully concrete, and fully human, expression as love. My aim here to read desire as love and love as desire. We can track this correlation developmentally. Desire in its earliest moments along the way of human development is an attachment to beloved objects. In Freud, the desire of infants is multiple and susceptible to many forms of satisfaction, but it is nevertheless oriented toward union with something beloved. When desire coalesces into normalized patterns of genital satisfaction during adolescence, and when it is sublimated so that people learn to find satisfaction in non-genital experiences, desire continues to be a way of being connected with a world or with certain objects within the world. But desire presses beyond any particular connection. It exceeds, first of all, its oedipalized or "normal" pattern. Something of primitive polyamorism resurfaces in desire: we experience inklings of fascination that tends to subvert patterns of the "normal." Desire is queering.

Desire's power to unsettle and transcend is not that it is capable of fixating on multiple objects, however. Instead, it is the restlessness of desire—its refusal to rest—that makes any object of satisfaction incomplete. In *The Confessions*, Augustine wrote that the human heart is restless until it rests in God.[20] However, resting in God—the figure of desire's final destination—is endlessly deferred because the restlessness that Augustine identified is not an accidental feature of the human but is the transcendent edge of human experience, the openness or incompleteness of human history, the endless stirring toward other and more that is embedded in the human heart, or the capacity to desire. Because desire as such can never be finally satisfied, because the structure of desire is to continually susceptible to re-opening, the "what" or the object of desire as such cannot be any conditioned object but must be unconditional.

Perhaps the appeal to Augustine makes it clear that this theology of culture and its account of the prophetic is rooted in an interpretation of human beings as certain types of creatures. Call it a "nature" if you will: it is a set of tendencies or capacities that characterize us a species. Human beings are erotic creatures who desire fulfillment and connection, and this *eros* is tinged with a sense of ultimacy or unconditionality. This is where the two requirements of a prophetic theology meet: the locus of the operation

20. Augustine, *Conf.* 1.1.

of transcendence points beyond itself. This transcending feature of *eros* is what Tillich called "ultimate concern"[21] and what John Caputo calls the unconditional[22] that stirs within every conditioned reality we experience, suffer, and enjoy. It is important to recognize that the unconditional can never be captured within a separate sphere or privileged locus of insight that is available to a select few or that is guarded by ecclesiastical authorities. It is, rather, but an edge or an opening within every sphere of human experience: traces of the unconditional are everywhere, even it is enclosed nowhere.

Again, I aim to link this desire to love. Desire for the unconditional is love because it seeks connection, serially, multiply, faithfully, during fleeting episodes or over the entire arc of a lifetime. Length of time offers no qualification, because any time is conditioned. Love reaches beyond. We love restlessly and endlessly within our limited capacities and vision. We recognize the unconditional within love when we experience the fact that longing endures, even amid the most fulfilling satisfactions. We long for objects that we can never fully reach, because no object can be fully reached, even those persons with whom we share decades of our lives. We long for a future that will not arrive. We long for a world we cannot achieve even though we are compelled by it, even though we feel its force of attraction.

But all this is perhaps too formal. If we are to avoid flying thousands of feet above the conflicts that cry out for prophecy, we must ask: What is the specific orientation of the unconditional? How does it dispose us? Is there a vector to restless desire, an itinerary that can be plotted, more or less? Here I draw on political theorist Jodi Dean, who argues in *The Communist Horizon* that there is a "collective desire for collectivity" that stirs within emancipatory social movements (She focuses on Occupy Wall Street in 2011.).[23] As I write, a month-long wave of massive street demonstrations protesting the murder of George Floyd is winding down, having forced new demands and even new vocabulary into popular awareness. It seems clear that the energy behind the demonstrations stemmed not only from anger at the atrocity of murder under the pressing knee of the police, and not only from horror at the violence of white supremacy that it exposed, but also from the pent-up desire for participation in a movement of collective solidarity and for emotional connection during a global COVID-19 pandemic and

21. Tillich, *Dynamics of Faith*, 1.
22. Caputo, *Weakness of God*, 84–86.
23. Dean, *Communist Horizon*, 157–59.

months of shutdown. I argue that Dean's collective desire for the collective suggests a vector or a trajectory that the desire for the unconditional takes that includes all these things. Love is oriented to connection with others and also to overcoming the oppression and violence that undermines or erodes human connections. Recalling Augustine, we might add that it is heightened in relationships with those who love as we love, especially if they love *what* we love. Collective desire is desire for collectivity, for the common. In other words, love is inherently a shared desire and it aims most fundamentally at sharing-itself. Though prophetic theology refuses to identify God with any existing object or series of objects, the image or trace of God within human experience is collective humanity as both object and subject, aim and agent, of desire: we desire *in* common and *for* the common.

An important question is, what is the relationship between the locus of transcendence and the openness or incompleteness of that locus? The common desire for the communal, or the shared desire for sharing, is a real human experience and a driver of real human agency, subject to all the distortions, misunderstandings, shortsightedness, etc., of any such motivation. And, of course, one of the ways it can be undermined is by trying to define itself too clearly or too definitely. The "collective" as subject and as object can be short-circuited by being identified with some narrower group or "collection." Those *with* whom we desire, the acknowledged bearers of desire, may be defined too narrowly, as in sectarian political formations; and those *for* whom we reach in desire, the range or scope of human well-being we seek to secure, can be too restrictive, as in social aims that are chauvinist, nationalist, or racist. The name of God, or the unconditional that stirs within the name, is in a dynamic relation to shared desire, continually breaking open the latter while driving its passion for wider and more inclusive collectivities. In fact, being broken open is how desire is preserved in its dynamism and protected from a process of ossification that would be its betrayal. Theology keeps calling and questioning and resisting closure, and that is how it may preserve desire in its desiring.

But the unconditional that prophetic theology seeks to attend also drives the passion of collective desire, because love desires embodiment and companionship. It is not enough to keep history open: we must be empowered to act, to commit ourselves to some living trajectory or to some discernible prospect for inclusive well-being. This means that, even though prophetic theology chastens the pretensions of historical actors and invites them to place their struggles in the widest possible series of considerations, it also urges us to struggle—or even, if need be, to fight. To be committed to a living trajectory is to have confidence that there is a discernible trace of love and grace in the world, something quite specific that can call us out of our comfort and into conflict with opposing historical forces, like Israel's rural tribes against the urban kings of Canaan. For Dean, the specific division that calls forth action is the communist horizon, a world-cleaving contest between those who offer their energies and their lives for a vision of common humanity and those forces, on the other hand, that are committed to the rule of private property, on the other. One may identify the "horizon" somewhat differently: for the axis of communism/Capitalism, one may substitute black liberation/white supremacy, or queerness/heteronormativity. Or there may be multiple horizons and therefore axes of conflict. If I read Dean correctly, she regards struggle for the common against the rule of property to be the general form of many such struggles and conflicts: all struggle against oppression is struggle for the common. The point, however, is that love as desire, and desire as love, drives us into commitment and conflict, even if we must acknowledge the fragility and the incompleteness of the outcomes of struggle.

This chapter has explored the valences of prophecy: what does prophecy say to human experiences embodied in social struggle, the arts and literatures? Anti-secularism is prophecy of the *"No."* We are not God, the Word thunders. Truth comes to us only as we are spoken to from beyond. We must resist self-congratulation and self-justification, and, above all, we must resist identifying anything within human experience (unless it is the church and its traditions) as a trace of God. Only in that way to do we escape the self-deceptions of immanence: capitalism, white supremacy, militarism, imperialism, death and destruction. Secularism, insofar as it summons itself to prophecy, is a prophecy of the *"Yes."* Truth is available to our experience. The transcendent is fully immanent. God is identifiable as a vanguard: the educated and civilized, the white-skinned, or else the abject, the rejected, the colonized, the dark-skinned. Whether in liberal or radical forms, secular prophecy affirms the human and clearly identifies its essence and its destiny. One defeats the demons by siding with the better angels. Finally, the theology of culture is a prophecy of the *"yes, And...."* Yes, traces of God are visible. The transcendent call to a different future resonates immanently within human experience as the contradiction between promise and reality. And, yet, it appears only as contradiction. Immanence is not complete. It remains permanently troubled: desire remains perpetually unsatisfied. The "And" is the "final" word—or, rather, it is the word that shakes all finalities.

What makes this third mode of prophecy even more radical than the radical option of anti-secularism is that it takes sides and enables judgment, plunging us deeper into social conflict rather than providing a route of escape into the merely transcendent. What makes if more radical than secular prophecy is that it resists closure and refuses to limit desire. This third kind of prophecy finds a stable magic, a dynamic that never ends or settles, locating the infinite within a finite that nevertheless cannot contain it. The commitment it engenders is therefore to the struggle and only secondarily to the vanguards—to that which speaks in the trace and only secondarily to the trace. By resisting closure, theological prophecy insists that revolt must continue: it insists on permanent revolution.

The Name of God and Secular Prophecy

But, once more, we must emphasize that, unlike theology as a field and as an arena of professionalized discourse, prophecy is anti-clerical. Part of its resistance to closure is its resistance to being made the preserve of a specially equipped class of thinkers. That is why it is important to stress, as a final point, that when the novelist or the activist, etc., discerns the unconditional, they are venturing into the very public, unpoliced realm of theological prophecy or prophetic theology. I have argued that theology as a discipline is oriented to the task of attending to this realm. In this somewhat attenuated sense, theology has something to add to the knowledge gained through secular prophetic speech and action (i.e, to what Robin D. G. Kelley calls the "new knowledge" gained in social struggle). Its knowledge is of a practical rather than a speculative sort: it arrives in the form of an admonition to keep desiring and keep hoping, and in a corresponding practical awareness that history is never closed and the struggle never complete. But, because of the peculiar qualities of the object of its attention, it is unable to grasp or capture its own truth and therefore it is not able to enforce rigid disciplinary boundaries. This prophetic edge of theology is therefore not a preserve of the qualified or a specialized body of knowledge.

Here is the place to try to do justice to Caputo's point that the name of God that is the rightful obsession of theology is infinitely translatable.[24]

24. Caputo, *Weakness of God*, 113–15.

This means that, even for theology, what is important is not the name, nor the logic in which the name is embedded (neither "God" nor theology *per se*), but, as Caputo says, the event that is harbored in the name. What is important is that the stirring and troubling of the orders of human community are attended, shepherded, and given voice, and that the event is not short-circuited or closed off from further stirring and troubling. Like the unruliness of desire itself, the prophetic surfaces and resurfaces in the midst of all kinds of struggles against what we might call, drawing once more on Freud, the reality principle, the order that is imposed by the current balance of forces in the world, an order that commands obedience and sacrifice. The struggle with this reality principle occurs not just in the imagination of religious visionaries, but also in the arts, in science, in politics, in social movements, and in many others. A theology of culture wants to say that the unconditional call for justice in all these realms is the prophetic soul of collective humanity.

Bibliography

Augustine, Saint. *Confessions*. Translated by Henry Chadwick. Oxford: Oxford University Press, 1991.
Babb, Sanora. *Whose Names Are Unknown*. Norman: University of Oklahoma Press, 2004.
Barth, Karl. *Barth in Conversation*. Vol. 1, *1959–1962*. Edited by Eberhard Busch. Louisville: Westminster John Knox, 2017.
———. *The Christian Life: Church Dogmatics IV, 4 Lecture Fragments*. Translated by Geoffrey W. Bromiley. Grand Rapids: Eerdmans, 1981.
———. *Church Dogmatics I/1: The Doctrine of the Word of God*. Translated by G. W. Bromiley. Edinburgh: T. & T. Clark, 1975.
———. *Church Dogmatics II/1: The Doctrine of God*. Translated by T. H. L. Parker et al. Edinburgh: T. & T. Clark, 1957.
———. *The Word of God and the Word of Man*. Translated by Douglas Horton. New York: Harper & Row, 1957.
Bellah, Robert N. "Civil Religion in America." *Daedalus* 134 (2005) 40–55. DOI: 10.1162/001152605774431464.
Bellah, Robert N., et al. *Habits of the Heart: Individualism and Commitment in American Life*. Berkeley: University of California Press, 2008.
Bercovitch, Sacvan. *The American Jeremiad*. Madison: University of Wisconsin Press, 1980.
———. *The Rites of Assent: Transformations in the Symbolic Construction of America*. New York: Routledge, 1993.
Berger, Dan, et al. "What Abolitionists Do." *Jacobin*, October 24, 2017. https://jacobinmag.com/2017/08/prison-abolition-reform-mass-incarceration.
Berger, Rose Marie. "A Cross of Human Bodies: How 71 Catholics Were Arrested for Protesting Immigrant Child Detention." *Sojourners*, July 25, 2019. https://sojo.net/articles/cross-human-bodies.
Blenkinsopp, Joseph. *A History of Prophecy in Israel*. Louisville: Westminster John Knox, 1996.
Blight, David W. *Frederick Douglass: Prophet of Freedom*. New York: Simon & Schuster, 2020.
Braunstein, Ruth. "Political Myopia and Prophetic Vision." *The Immanent Frame*, March 12, 2018. http://tif.ssrc.org/2018/03/12/political-myopia-and-prophetic-vision/.
———. *Prophets and Patriots: Faith in Democracy across the Political Divide*. Oakland: University of California Press, 2017.

Bibliography

Brown, Adrienne Maree. *Emergent Strategy: Shaping Change, Changing Worlds.* Chico, CA: AK Press, 2017.

Brown, Adrienne Maree, and Walidah Imarisha, eds. *Octavia's Brood: Science Fiction Stories from Social Justice Movements.* Chico, CA: AK Press, 2015.

Brueggemann, Walter. *Inscribing the Text: Sermons and Prayers of Walter Brueggemann.* Edited by Anna Carter Florence. Minneapolis: Fortress, 2004.

———. *The Prophetic Imagination.* 2nd ed. Minneapolis: Fortress, 2001.

Buber, Martin. *The Prophetic Faith.* New York: Harper & Row, 1960.

Bullard, Robert D. "Differential Vulnerabilities: Environmental and Economic Inequality and Government Response to Unnatural Disasters." *Social Research* 75 (2008) 753–84.

Caputo, John D. *The Weakness of God: A Theology of the Event.* Bloomington: Indiana University Press, 2006.

Carter, Brandon. "Jon Stewart Blasts Lawmakers in Hearing for Sept. 11 Victim Compensation Fund." *NPR*, June 11, 2019. https://www.npr.org/2019/06/11/731706492/jon-stewart-blasts-lawmakers-in-hearing-for-sept-11-victim-compensation.

Chappell, David L. *A Stone of Hope: Prophetic Religion and the Death of Jim Crow.* Chapel Hill: University of North Carolina Press, 2004.

"Chief Plenty Coups." https://www.nps.gov/bica/learn/historyculture/chief-plenty-coups.htm.

Clark, Christopher W. "What Comes to the Surface: Storms, Bodies, and Community in Jesmyn Ward's *Salvage the Bones.*" *Mississippi Quarterly: The Journal of Southern Cultures* 68 (2015) 341–58.

Coleman, Monica. *Making a Way Out of No Way: A Womanist Theology.* Minneapolis: Fortress, 2008.

Cone, James. *Black Theology and Black Power.* New York: Harper & Row, 1969.

Coronado, Raúl. *A World Not to Come: A History of Latino Writing and Print Culture.* Cambridge: Harvard University Press, 2016.

Crownshaw, Rick. "A Natural History of Testimony." In *the Future of Testimony: Interdisciplinary Perspective on Witnessing*, edited by Jane Kilby and Antony Rowland, 160–76. New York: Routledge, 2014.

Dalamangas, Rachel Cole. "Interview: T. Geronimo Johnson." *Zingmagazine*, December 2012. www.zingmagazine.com/drupal/node/6712.

Darsey, James. *Prophetic Tradition and Radical Rhetoric in America.* New York: New York University Press, 1999.

Davis, Ellen F. *Biblical Prophecy: Perspectives for Christian Theology, Discipleship, and Ministry.* Interpretation Series. Louisville: Westminster John Knox, 2014.

Dean, Jodi. *The Communist Horizon.* New York: Verso, 2012.

Delany, Samuel R. *Aye, and Gomorrah: Stories.* New York: Vintage, 2003.

———. *Heavenly Breakfast: An Essay on the Winter of Love.* 1979. Reprint, Flint, MI: Bamberger, 1997.

———. *The Motion of Light in Water: Sex and Science Fiction Writing in the East Village.* 1988. Reprint, Minneapolis: University of Minnesota Press, 2004.

———. *Times Square Red, Times Square Blue.* New York: New York University Press, 1999.

Denetdale, Jennifer. "Chairmen, Presidents, and Princesses: The Navajo Nation, Gender, and the Politics of Tradition." *Wicazo Sa Review* 21 (2006) 9–28. DOI: 10.1353/wic.2006.0004.

Bibliography

Donica, Joseph. "Disaster's Ethics of Literature: Voicing Katrina's Stories in a Digital Age." In *Ten Years after Katrina: Critical Perspectives of the Storm's Effect on American Culture and Identity*, edited by Glenn Jellenik and Mary Ruth Marotte, 3–16. Lanham, MD: Lexington, 2015.

Duke, Marshall. "The Stories That Bind Us: What Are the Twenty Questions?" *Huffington Post*, March 23, 2013. http://www.huffingtonpost.com/marshall-p-duke/the-stories-that-bind-us-_b_2918975.html.

Dyson, Michael Eric. *Come Hell or High Water: Hurricane Katrina and the Color of Disaster*. New York: Basic Civitas, 2006.

Edwards, Erica R. *Charisma and the Fictions of Black Leadership*. Minneapolis: University of Minnesota Press, 2012.

Ellison, Ralph. "Living with Music." In *Shadow and Act*, 187–98. New York: Random House, 1964.

Feiler, Bruce. "The Stories That Bind Us." *New York Times*, March 15, 2013. https://www.nytimes.com/2013/03/17/fashion/the-family-stories-that-bind-us-this-life.html.

Fornoff, Erin. "Gary Birdsong: Preaching to the Converted." *Daily Tar Heel*, November 7, 2001. https://www.dailytarheel.com/article/2001/11/gary_birdsong_preaching_to_the_converted.

Freedman, Carl. "Samuel Delany: A Biographical and Critical Overview." In *A Companion to Science Fiction*, edited by David Seed, 398–407. Malden, MA: Blackwell, 2005.

Friedman, Leah. "Greta Thunberg to Attend New York Climate Talks. She'll Take a Sailboat." *New York Times*, July 29, 2019. https://www.nytimes.com/2019/07/29/climate/greta-thunberg-sailing-climate-summit.html.

Frymer-Kensky, Tikva. *Reading the Women of the Bible*. New York: Schocken, 2002.

Gafney, Wilda C. *Daughters of Miriam: Women Prophets in Ancient Israel*. Minneapolis: Fortress, 2008.

Genesis Rabbah. *Midrash Rabbah*. Edited by H. Freedman and Maurice Simon. London: Soncino, 1961. https://ia800500.us.archive.org/13/items/RabbaGenesis/midrashrabbahgen027557mbp.pdf.

Gilbert, Kenyatta. "What Does It Mean to Be Prophetic Today?" *Sojourners*, 2018. https://sojo.net/media/what-does-it-mean-be-prophetic-today.

Gilmore, Ruth Wilson. *Golden Gulag: Prisons, Surplus, Crisis, and Opposition in Globalizing California*. Berkeley: University of California Press, 2007.

Goldenberg, David M. "What Did Ham Do to Noah?" In *"The Words of a Wise Man's Mouth Are Gracious" (Qoh 10,12): Festschrift for Gunter Stemberger on the Occasion of His 65th Birthday*, edited by Mauro Perani, 257–65. Berlin: de Gruyter, 2005.

Gottwald, Norman K. *The Tribes of Yahweh: A Sociology of the Religion of Liberated Israel, 1250-1050 B.C.E.* Maryknoll, NY: Orbis, 1979.

Gregory, James N. "The Dust Bowl Migration." In *Poverty in the United States: An Encyclopedia of History, Politics, and Policy*, edited by Gwendolyn Mink and Alice O'Connor, 242–48. Santa Barbara, CA: ABC-Clio, 2004. http://faculty.washington.edu/gregoryj/dust%20bowl%20migration.htm.

Gutiérrez, Gustavo. *A Theology of Liberation: History, Politics, and Salvation*. Translated by Sister Caridad Inda and John Eagleson. Rev. ed. Maryknoll, NY: Orbis, 1988.

Harney, Stefano, and Fred Moten. *The Undercommons: Fugitive Planning and Black Studies*. Wivenhoe, UK: Autonomedia, 2013.

Hartman, Saidiya V. *Scenes of Subjection: Terror, Slavery, and Self-Making in Nineteenth-Century America*. New York: Oxford University Press, 1997.

Bibliography

Hauerwas, Stanley. *Against the Nations: War and Survival in a Liberal Society*. Notre Dame: University of Notre Dame Press, 1992.

Hertsgaard, Mark, and Kyle Pope. "The Media Are Complacent While the World Burns." *Columbia Journalism Review*, April 22, 2019. https://www.cjr.org/special_report/climate-change-media.php.

Heschel, Abraham Joshua. *The Prophets: An Introduction*. New York: Harper, 1962.

The Intergovernmental Panel on Climate Change. "Special Report: Global Warming of 1.5° C." https://www.ipcc.ch/sr15/.

James, C. L. R., et al. *Facing Reality*. Detroit: Beckwick, 1974.

Johnson, Glenn S., and Shirley A. Rainey. "Hurricane Katrina: Public Health and Environmental Justice Issues Front and Centered." *Race, Gender & Class* 14 (2007) 17–37.

Johnson, T. Geronimo. *Hold It 'Til It Hurts*. Minneapolis: Coffee House, 2012.

"Journalism, Satire, or Just Laughs? 'The Daily Show with Jon Stewart' Examined." https://www.journalism.org/2008/05/08/journalism-satire-or-just-laughs-the-daily-show-with-jon-stewart-examined/

Joustra, Robert, and Alissa Wilkinson. *How to Survive the Apocalypse: Zombies, Cylons, Faith, and Politics at the End of the World*. Grand Rapids: Eerdmans, 2016.

Kaufman, Gordon D. *In Face of Mystery: A Constructive Theology*. Cambridge: Harvard University Press, 1993.

Kaveny, Cathleen. *Prophecy without Contempt: Religious Discourse in the Public Square*. Cambridge: Harvard University Press, 2016.

Keeling, K. "Looking for M—: Queer Temporality, Black Political Possibility, and Poetry from the Future." *GLQ: A Journal of Lesbian and Gay Studies* 15 (2009) 565–82. DOI: 10.1215/10642684-2009-002.

Kelle, Brad E. "The Phenomenon of Israelite Prophecy in Contemporary Scholarship." *Currents in Biblical Research* 12 (2014) 275–320.

Kelley, Robin D. G. *Freedom Dreams: The Black Radical Imagination*. Boston: Beacon, 2002.

Kim, Catherine. "The Senate Just Extended the September 11th Victim Compensation Fund through 2090." *Vox*, July 23, 2019. https://www.vox.com/2019/7/23/20704064/september-11-victim-compensation-fund-extended-senate.

King, Martin Luther, Jr. *I Have a Dream: Writings and Speeches that Changed World*. Edited by James Melvin Washington. New York: HarperOne, 1992.

———. "I See the Promised Land." http://www.edchange.org/multicultural/speeches/mlk_promised_land.html.

Lambelet, Kyle. *¡Presente! Nonviolent Politics and the Resurrection of the Dead*. Washington, DC: Georgetown University Press, 2020.

Lapsley, Jacqueline. *Whispering the Word: Hearing Women's Stories in the Old Testament*. Louisville: Westminster John Knox, 2005.

LaRocque, Emma. *When the Other Is Me: Native Resistance Discourse, 1850–1990*. Winnipeg: University of Manitoba Press, 2010.

Lear, Jonathan. *Radical Hope: Ethics in the Face of Cultural Devastation*. Cambridge: Harvard University Press, 2006.

"Life-history of Rabbi Arthur Waskow." https://theshalomcenter.org/life-history-rabbi-arthur-waskow.

Lindahl, Carl. "Publishing Up a Storm: Katrina Book Notes." *Callaloo* 29 (2006) 1543–48. http://www.jstor.org/stable/4488499.

Bibliography

Linebaugh, Peter, and Marcus Rediker. *The Many-Headed Hydra: Sailors, Slaves, Commoners, and the Hidden History of the Revolutionary Atlantic*. London: Verso, 2000.

Lloyd, Christopher. "Creaturely, Throwaway Life after Katrina: *Salvage the Bones* and *Beasts of the Southern Wild*." *South: A Scholarly Journal* 48 (2016) 246–64.

Lloyd, Vincent. "Black Religion as Black Radicalism." *Black Agenda Report*, August 30, 2017. https://www.blackagendareport.com/black-religion-black-radicalism.

———. *The Religion of the Field Negro: On Black Secularism and Black Theology*. New York: Fordham University Press, 2018.

Locke, Mamie E. "Of Fury and Furies: Female Roles in Salvage the Bones." *Notes on American Literature* 22 (2013) 12–19.

Lopez, Viviana. "Campus Preachers A Controversial Staple at Colleges Nationwide." *USA Today*, October 21, 2011. https://www.usatoday.com/story/college/2011/10/21/campus-preaches-a-controversial-staple-at-colleges-nationwide/37387213/.

Lowe, Lisa. *The Intimacies of Four Continents*. Durham: Duke University Press, 2015.

Lyons, Scott Richard. *X-Marks: Native Signatures of Assent*. Minneapolis: University of Minnesota Press, 2010.

Mann, Regis. "Theorizing 'What Could Have Been': Black Feminism, Historical Memory, and the Politics of Reclamation." *Women's Studies* 40 (2011) 575–99. DOI: 10.1080/00497878.2011.581564.

Marotte, Mary Ruth. "Pregnancies, Storms, and Legacies of Loss in Jesmyn Ward's *Salvage the Bones*." In *Ten Years after Katrina: Critical Perspectives of the Storm's Effect on American Culture and Identity*, edited by Glenn Jellenik and Mary Ruth Marotte, 207–19. Lanham, MD: Lexington, 2015.

Marotte, Mary Ruth, and Glenn Jellenik. "Introduction: Reading Hurricane Katrina." In *Ten Years after Katrina: Critical Perspectives of the Storm's Effect on American Culture and Identity*, edited by Glenn Jellenik and Mary Ruth Marotte, vii–xiv. Lanham, MD: Lexington, 2015.

Martínez, M. E. "Archives, Bodies, and Imagination: The Case of Juana Aguilar and Queer Approaches to History, Sexuality, and Politics." *Radical History Review* 120 (2014) 159–82. DOI: 10.1215/01636545-2703787.

Mathewes, Charles T., and Christopher McKnight Nichols. *Prophesies of Godlessness: Predictions of America's Imminent Secularization, from the Puritans to the Present Day*. Oxford: Oxford University Press, 2008.

McGrath, Matt. "Climate Change: 12 Years to Save the Planet? Make that 18 Months." *BBC News*, July 23, 2019. https://www.bbc.com/news/science-environment-48964736.

Milbank, John. *Theology and Social Theory: Beyond Secular Reason*. 2nd ed. Oxford: Wiley-Blackwell, 2006.

Miller, Patrick D. "The Good Neighborhood: Identity and Community through the Commandments." In *Character and Scripture: Moral Formation, Community, and Biblical Interpretation*, edited by William P. Brown, 55–72. Grand Rapids: Eerdmans, 2002.

Morris, Cherise. "On Trans and Queer Prison Abolition and Sustaining Movements: An Interview with Eric A. Stanley." *Bluestockings Magazine*, April 6, 2017. http://bluestockingsmag.com/2015/06/22/on-trans-and-queer-prison-abolition-and-sustaining-movements-an-interview-with-eric-a-stanley/.

Morrison, Toni. *Jazz*. 1992. Reprint, New York: Vintage, 2004.

Bibliography

Murphy, Andrew R. *Prodigal Nation: Moral Decline and Divine Punishment from New England to 9/11*. New York: Oxford University Press, 2010.

Niebuhr, Reinhold. *Essays in Applied Christianity*. Edited by D. B. Robertson. New York: Meridian, 1959.

———. "Why Is Barth Silent on Hungary?" In *Essays in Applied Christianity*, by Reinhold Niebuhr, edited by D. B. Robertson, 183–90. New York: Meridian, 1959.

Nixon, Lindsay. "Visual Cultures of Indigenous Futurism." In *Otherwise Worlds: Against Settle Colonialism and Anti-blackness*, edited by Tiffany Lethabo King et al., 332–42. Durham: Duke University Press, 2020.

Nyong'o, Tavia. "Back to the Garden: Queer Ecology in Samuel Delany's *Heavenly Breakfast*." *American Literary History* 24 (2012) 747–67.

Oakes, James. *The Radical and the Republican: Frederick Douglass, Abraham Lincoln, and the Triumph of Antislavery*. New York: Norton, 2008.

O'Connor, Kathleen M. *Jeremiah: Pain and Promise*. Minneapolis: Fortress, 2011.

Olson, Dennis. *Numbers*. Interpretation. Louisville: Westminster John Knox, 1996.

Oppenheimer, Mark. "Jon Stewart, Religion Teacher Extraordinaire." https://religionandpolitics.org/2012/05/01/jon-stewart-religion-teacher-extraordinaire/.

Pettit, Phillip. *Republicanism: A Theory of Freedom and Government*. Oxford: Oxford University Press, 1999.

"Pit Preacher Moves off His Stage after Conflict, Appeals Citation." *Carolina Alumni Review*, March 23, 2007. https://alumni.unc.edu/news/pit-preacher-moves-off-his-stage-after-conflict-appeals-citation/.

Prothero, Stephen. *The American Bible: How Our Words Unite, Divide, and Define a Nation*. New York: HarperOne, 2012.

Putnam, Robert D., et al. *American Grace: How Religion Divides and Unites Us*. New York: Simon & Schuster Paperbacks, 2012.

Raboteau, Albert J. *American Prophets: Seven Religious Radicals and Their Struggle for Social and Political Justice*. Princeton: Princeton University Press, 2016.

Rad, Gerhard von. *The Message of the Prophets*. London: SCM, 1982.

Rankine, Claudia. "The Condition of Black Life Is One of Mourning." In *The Fire This Time: A New Generation Speaks about Race*, edited by Jesmyn Ward, 145–55. New York: Scribner's, 2016.

Redmond, Shana. *Everything Man: The Form and Function of Paul Robeson*. Durham: Duke University Press, 2020.

Roberts, William Clare. *Marx's Inferno: The Political Theory of "Capital."* Princeton: Princeton University Press, 2017.

Rodriguez, Dylan. *Forced Passages: Imprisoned Radical Intellectuals and the U.S. Prison Regime*. Minneapolis: University of Minnesota Press, 2006.

Rojas, Paula X. "Are the Cops in Our Heads and Hearts?" In *The Revolution Will Not Be Funded: Beyond the Non-profit Industrial Complex*, edited by INCITE!, 197–214. Durham: Duke University Press, 2017.

Saad, Lydia. "Americans as Concerned as Ever about Global Warming." *Gallup*, March 25, 2019. https://news.gallup.com/poll/248027/americans-concerned-ever-global-warming.aspx.

Sailiata, Kirisitina. "Decolonization." In *Native Studies Keywords*, edited by Stephanie Nohelani Teves et al., 301–7. Tucson: University of Arizona Press, 2015.

Schellenberg, Annette. "An Anti-Prophet among the Prophets? On the Relationship of Jonah to Prophecy." *Journal for the Study of the Old Testament* 39 (2015) 353–71.

Bibliography

Schneidau, Herbert N. *Sacred Discontent: The Bible and Western Tradition*. Berkeley: University of California Press, 1977.
Scott, Darieck. "Delany's Divinities." *American Literary History* 24 (2012) 702–22.
Scott, Joan. "The Evidence of Experience." *Critical Inquiry* 17 (1991) 773–97.
Scranton, Roy. *Learning to Die in the Anthropocene*. San Francisco: City Lights, 2015.
Serpell, Namwali. "The Banality of Empathy." *The New York Review of Books*, March 2, 2019. https://www.nybooks.com/daily/2019/03/02/the-banality-of-empathy/.
Sharp, Carolyn. *Old Testament Prophets for Today*. Louisville: Westminster John Knox, 2009.
Shulman, George. *American Prophecy: Race and Redemption in American Political Culture*. Minneapolis: University of Minnesota Press, 2008.
Smith, James K. A. "Join the Anti-Revolutionary Party." *Comment Magazine*, Fall 2016. https://www.cardus.ca/comment/article/editorial-join-the-anti-revolutionary-party/.
Smith, Kenneth L., and Ira G. Zepp Jr. "Martin Luther King's Vision of the Beloved Community." *Christian Century*, April 3, 1974.
Smith, Ted. *Weird John Brown: Divine Violence and the Limits of Ethics*. Stanford: Stanford University Press, 2014.
Solnit, Rebecca. *A Paradise Built in Hell: The Extraordinary Communities That Arise in Disaster*. New York: Penguin, 2009.
Sommer, Doris. *The Work of Art in the World*. Durham: Duke University Press, 2014.
Spade, Dean. *Normal Life: Administrative Violence, Critical Trans Politics, and the Limits of Law*. Durham: Duke University Press, 2015.
Steinbeck, John. *The Grapes of Wrath*. New York: Penguin, 2006.
Stewart, Jon. "Statement to the House Judiciary Committee on the September 11th Victim Compensation Fund." https://www.americanrhetoric.com/speeches/jonstewart911firstresponders.htm.
Stulman, Louis, and Hyun Chul Paul Kim. *You Are My People: An Introduction to Prophetic Literature*. Nashville: Abingdon, 2010.
Taylor, Charles. *A Secular Age*. Cambridge: Belknap Press of Harvard University Press, 2007.
Taylor, Fred Barney, dir. *The Polymath, or, The Life and Opinions of Samuel R. Delany, Gentleman*. Maestro Media, 2009.
Teves, Stephanie Nohelani, et al., eds. *Native Studies Keywords*. Tucson: University of Arizona Press, 2015.
Thunberg, Greta. "School Strike for Climate—Save the World by Changing the Rules." *TED*, November 2018. https://www.ted.com/talks/greta_thunberg_school_strike_for_climate_save_the_world_by_changing_the_rules?language=en.
Tillich, Paul. *Biblical Religion and the Search for Ultimate Reality*. Chicago: University of Chicago Press, 1964.
———. *Dynamics of Faith*. New York: Harper, 1958.
———. *The Shaking of the Foundations*. New York: Scribner's, 1948.
Trethewey, Natasha. *Beyond Katrina: A Meditation on the Mississippi Gulf Coast*. Athens: University of Georgia Press, 2010.
Trible, Phyllis. "Bringing Miriam Out of the Shadows." *Bible Review* 5 (1989) 14–25, 34.
Viego, Antonio. *Dead Subjects: Toward a Politics of Loss in Latino Studies*. Durham: Duke University Press, 2008.

Waldman, Scott. "Trump Administration Officials Scrubbed Climate Change from Releases." *Scientific American*, July 8, 2019. https://www.scientificamerican.com/article/trump-administration-officials-scrubbed-climate-change-from-press-releases/.
Walzer, Michael. *Exodus and Revolution*. New York: Basic Books, 1985.
———. *In God's Shadow: Politics in the Hebrew Bible*. New Haven: Yale University Press, 2012.
———. *Interpretation and Social Criticism*. Cambridge: Harvard University Press, 1993.
———. *The Revolution of the Saints: A Study in the Origins of Radical Politics*. Cambridge: Harvard University Press, 1990.
Ward, Jesmyn. *Salvage the Bones*. New York: Bloomsbury, 2011.
———. "We Do Not Swim in Our Cemeteries." *The Oxford American* 62 (2008) 34–41.
Warren, Calvin L. *Ontological Terror: Blackness, Nihilism, and Emancipation*. Durham: Duke University Press, 2018.
Warrior, Robert Allen. "Canaanites, Cowboys, and Indians: Deliverance, Conquest, and Liberation Theology Today." *Christianity and Crisis*, September 11, 1989. https://www.rmselca.org/sites/rmselca.org/files/media/canaanites_cowboys_and_indians.pdf.
Waskow, Arthur. "Blocking 'ICE' HQ in Washington DC." https://theshalomcenter.org/content/blocking-ice-hq-washington-dc.
Weber, Max. *Ancient Judaism*. Translated by Don Martindale and Hans H. Gerth. New York: Free Press, 1967.
———. "Politics as a Vocation." In *From Max Weber: Essays in Sociology*, translated and edited by H. H. Gerth and C. Wright Mills, 89–140. New York: Routledge, 2014.
Weheliye, Alexander G. *Habeas Viscus: Racializing Assemblages, Biopolitics, and Black Feminist Theories of the Human*. Durham: Duke University Press, 2014.
West, Cornel. *Prophetic Fragments: Illuminations of the Crisis in American Religion and Culture*. Grand Rapids: Eerdmans, 1993.
West, Cornel, and Christa Buschendorf. *Cornel West on Black Prophetic Fire*. Boston: Beacon, 2014.
Wilder, Gary. *Freedom Time: Negritude, Decolonization, and the Future of the World*. Durham: Duke University Press, 2015.
Wilderson, Frank. *Red, White, and Black: Cinema and the Structure of U.S. Antagonisms*. Durham: Duke University Press, 2010.
Willis, Amy. "How to Be a Prophet: Models of Prophetic Discourse." Unpublished lecture given at Wilson College, Chambersburg, Pennsylvania, September 2, 2014.
———. "'Once There Were Two Men': The Prophetic Story and the Moral Imagination." Lecture, Fiftieth Annual Orr Forum, Chambersburg, Pennsylvania, September 2014.
Wallis, Jim. "The Truth Smirks (Extended Interview Content)." *Sojourners*, July 2009. https://sojo.net/magazine/july-2009/truth-smirks-extended-interview-content?action=magazine.article&issue=soj0907&article=the-truth-smirks&0907_webextra=Extended%20Format.
Wolin, Sheldon. "Fugitive Democracy." *Constellations* 1 (1994) 11–25.
Zimmerman, Leda. "What the Prisoner's Dilemma Tells Us about Climate Change." https://www.weforum.org/agenda/2018/06/the-moral-calculus-of-climate-change.

Contributors

John Elia is Associate Professor and Thérèse Murray Goodwin '49 Chair in Philosophy at Wilson College. His recent work includes "Postnatural Comedy in Last Man on Earth" in *Apocalypse TV* and other essays in popular culture and philosophy.

Tom James is pastor of Eastminster United Presbyterian Church in Toledo, Ohio. He is the author of *Becoming-Buddhist, and-Jewish, and Possibly-Catholic: A Spirituality of Divine Madness*; *In Face of Reality: The Constructive Theology of Gordon D. Kaufman*; and coauthor of *A Philosophy of Christian Materialism*.

Vincent W. Lloyd is Associate Professor of Theology and Religious Studies at Villanova University. His books include *The Problem with Grace*, *Black Natural Law*, and a coedited volume, *Race and Secularism in America*.

George Shulman is Professor of Political Theory at the Gallatin School, New York University.

Roberto Sirvent is Associate Professor of Political and Social Ethics at Hope International University in Fullerton, California. He is the author of the book *Embracing Vulnerability: Human and Divine*.

Andrea Smith is Associate Professor of Ethnic Studies at University of California, Riverside and author of *Native Americans and the Christian Right: The Gendered Politics of Unlikely Alliances* and the forthcoming *Unreconciled: The Christian Right and Racial Reconciliation*.

Amy Merrill Willis is Associate Professor of Religious Studies at the University of Lynchburg. She is also the author of *Dissonance and the Drama of Divine Sovereignty in the Book of Daniel* and a contributor to the *Women's Bible Commentary*, 3rd ed. and the *New Oxford Annotated Study Bible*, 5th ed.

CONTRIBUTORS

Lisa Woolley is Professor of English at Wilson College. She is the author of *American Voices of the Chicago Renaissance*, "Racial and Ethnic Semiosis in Mitsuye Yamada's 'Mrs. Higashi Is Dead,'" "Vachel Lindsay's Crusade for Cultural Literacy," "From Chicago Renaissance to Chicago Renaissance: The Poetry of Fenton Johnson," "Two Chicago Renaissances with Harlem between Them," and "Richard Wright's Dogged Pursuit of His Place in the Natural World."

www.ingramcontent.com/pod-product-compliance
Lightning Source LLC
Chambersburg PA
CBHW061452300426
44114CB00014B/1943